ROOM N·9

LESSONS OF LIFE FROM BEHIND THE CLASSROOM DOOR

LARRY SHURILLA

DIGITAL LEGEND

© 2022 by Larry Shurilla

All rights reserved. No part of this publication may be reproduced or transmitted in any form or by any means, graphic, electronic or mechanical, including photocopying, recording, taping or information storage and retrieval systems, without written permission from the author.

Published by:
Digital Legend Press
Salt Lake City UT

801-810-7718
info@digitalegend.com

ISBN: 978-1-937735-30-2

Cover design: Jerry Higgins
Editor: Jim Martyka

Printed in the United States of America

*For the joy we see in those faces we teach each day
and the hope we won't see certain faces at night.*

PRAISE FOR THE AUTHOR OF *ROOM N-9*

"Larry's ability to uncover broadly applicable insights from a school environment, coupled with his compelling writing style— simple yet profound; with both pathos and humor, and all in between—will grab the attention of anyone from one aspiring to teach, an incumbent teacher, a student, a school principle, a house-wife, a businessman, and even to a corporate president. "

—Dr. D. H. (Dee) Groberg, Founder and Vice President of International Operations at Franklin-Covey Consultants

"You brought to life the middle school classrooms and life of these young people. You also give such an honest picture of being a teacher for many years. This is a valuable read for any current teacher, but also important for any future educator to read and comprehend. I have to say there was great emotion in 'Uncle Larry' and in the 'Flying Tank.'"

—Dr. Keith Marty, Superintendent Parkway School District, St. Louis, Missouri

"I've known Larry Shurilla for over 30 years and whenever I get together with him I can always count on hearing a great story. I was excited to finally read Larry's classroom and coaching stories as well as his teacher escapades in the middle school where I once held a basketball clinic with his 6th grade classes. Larry has the ability to turn a walk down the canned food aisle of a grocery store into a memorable and classic story."

—Fred Roberts, 12-year NBA Veteran and Educator

"A must read for anyone in the world of education. *Room N-9: Lessons of Life From Behind the Classroom Door* will have you running the gamut of emotions from pure laughter and joy to gratitude and compassion for all that is the profession of teaching. A truly rare peak at the rollercoaster ride that is education and the amazing impact a teacher can have on so many."

—Cathy Kaiser-Drago, K-12 Instructional Coach, Hamilton School District, Sussex, Wisconsin

CONTENTS

Introduction 1

Becky 4

Winning Is No More Than This 7

Jackpot! 13

Trojans! Trojans! Trojans! 15

When the Hand Goes Up 16

If God Were Here Right Now 20

Rambo 22

The Heart of a Champion 24

Uncle Larry 28

Live Long And Prosper 31

Fiddling About 36

Broken Arrow 39

The Last Race 42

The Flying Tank 45

The Color of Breath 48

And the Oscar Goes To 50

Take a Knee 52

Today Is a Free Day 55

Survival 57

Custodians of Education 59

The Elephant Man Diary 67

Castle Wolfenstein 70

The Luckiest Man 77

Bus Rides 87

Shurilla Gorilla Awards. 93

PTC. 96

Ranger Rick-Rolled 102

The Mantis Parable. 106

Standardized Testing. 110

The Twelve Days of Middle School Christmas 114

Shop Talk 117

One Last Look 119

Epilogue. 124

ACKNOWLEDGEMENTS

I would like to thank my wife, Kathy, my family and all my teacher friends for the support and love they've given me throughout my years of teaching. I also thank Jim Martyka for his editing, guidance and encouragement. I especially thank my students for the privilege of being their teacher. If we ever chance to meet in the future, please stop me, say hello and tell me what you're up to! I'm terrible at remembering names, but I will never forget you and the time we shared in Room N-9.

INTRODUCTION

The day will come to every classroom teacher, when he or she will take that final walk through their classroom. I'm not talking about the walk-through at the end of the school year, when everyone gets ready for summer. That blitzkrieg happens every year with textbook check-ins, bulletin board dismantling, backing up computer files, and stashing of desk minutia. No, I'm talking about the Final Walk-Through—the *retirement* walk-through, when you really won't be back in that room you called home for X number of years.

In my case, it was a thirty-one-year goodbye.

I begin writing this reverie of my teaching career about three months after that final walk-through. The early September sun is beginning to set and I feel the time is right—while the memories are still fresh and school bus drivers are practicing their new routes—to put down in writing some of the most memorable days of my teaching career.

Teaching is a somewhat unique profession in that it has such a distinctive beginning and ending each school year! You meet students for the first time in August or September, spend nearly every day by their side for 10 months and then, poof! They're off to summer vacation and the next school year, the next teacher, the next stage of growth. They may move on, but they are never forgotten. The year we spent together in Room N-9 has forever changed me and hopefully, in a positive way, the kids I was fortunate enough to teach.

Every occupation has lessons to learn, but in the teaching profession our job *is* to teach lessons! Every day we plan best how to teach curricula in math, science, social studies, English, reading and writing. We may also formally teach lessons about civics, determination, planning, creativity, vision, inclusion and logic. And then something magical happens. Sometimes life has an unplanned lesson waiting for us to discover, together, teacher and student, behind the classroom door.

I am not naïve enough, nor experienced enough, to claim that teaching is any more difficult than any of a host of demanding professions. All I can share is my personal experiences that teaching is often tough and sometimes sublime. In the public school, some days may not be Omaha Beach rough, but society's problems do not stay at home. They come to school too. Being a classroom teacher is a front-line occupation and some of my stories are raw, because they're real and some of them are beautiful, because the human spirit cannot be suppressed. You'll have a hard time believing some of these events actually occurred, but I assure you, they did.

I used to kid with my son that my personal "teacher's hell" would consist of a private viewing room, wherein I was strapped to a chair and forced to face a video screen that displayed spliced classroom scenes from every student I ignored in my teaching career! As other teachers returned from Satan's video booth, we would all ask each other, "How long was yours?" I really tried not to ignore students when they wanted to share the news about their new hamster, or where they went over the weekend, or the game they won or lost, but we all know there comes a time when the other twenty-seven are waiting and restless while we're trying to accommodate the one!

Teaching can also be a peek into heaven because working with children is God's choicest profession and oftentimes those few minutes we give to the one connects us in a beautiful way, forever. There is no more rewarding feeling for a teacher than when a student looks into your eyes and you know, they get it! Learning has sprouted in his or her mind and they feel the intrinsic worth of understanding, accomplishment and personal growth.

Teaching is life. We even become part of family discussions at the dinner table for a school year and sometimes more. "Mr. Shurilla ripped his pants on the playground today, Dad! (Really happened!) Oh, Mom, Mr. Shurilla said he was ready for the nut house after teaching our class today!" Well, hopefully, they'll mention something about math or science once in a while, too!

This writing will not be strictly chronological. Rather, as I think back on all those years of teaching, certain events will come to mind and I'll share them to the best of my recollection. Also, I'm changing all the school-related individual proper-names, except my own! No one need fear, neither students nor fellow teachers, that I am talking about them! Of course, I *will be* talking about them, but I won't be using their actual names and no one will know for sure.

If you're a teacher and your classroom is anything like mine, I'm sure you could tell a story or two about the mementos you have cluttering your desk or plastering your walls. Oops, excuse me, not plastering. Masking tape or anything that really works on the walls was disallowed in my school years ago. Only blue painter's tape or perhaps, the gummy stuff you roll into little balls is allowed now. Okay, first confession: when my posters kept falling down for the fifth time after two weeks of school, I may have enlisted a roll of grey duct tape to permanently cement those periodic table charts and Snoopy inspirations onto the white classroom walls of sixth grade Room N-9. Phew! Glad I got that off my chest . . but you won't get it off my walls.

I spent my entire teaching career at the same school, Templeton Middle School, just outside of Milwaukee, Wisconsin in the Hamilton School District. I taught anywhere from fifth to eighth grades during my career, but the vast majority in sixth grade. My first ten years, I taught all subjects as a Learning Disabilities teacher, then spent the remaining twenty-one years as a regular education, sixth grade teacher. Aside from teaching, I coached track and field and cross country for over twenty-five years.

While I think anyone interested in chuckling, crying, observing, or relating to the human experience will enjoy reading this book, I found that I was often thinking of new teachers as I wrote, envying them for the adventure that awaits, and wanting in some very small way to impart lessons that have sunk into my muskmelon of a head. You will find the stories presented are universal to the teaching profession. While new teachers will gain insights into what to do and what not to do in the classroom, veteran teachers will enjoy the ride, find encouragement, and be reminded why they became teachers in the first place.

Room N-9 holds stories of struggling kids, achieving kids, wacky teachers, surprising classroom moments, inspiring coaching messages, and once-in-a-lifetime lessons. Ultimately, the spirit of middle school education and the love of a teacher for his students fills every page.

In the end, these stories are *my* mementos, the ones I felt worth sharing. They line the walls of my heart and are gently placed on the desktop of my soul, where I can take a quick peek or pause and hold them dear, remembering the faces and stories of my kids and friends who shared their lives with me.

Now get going and start reading! I've just cracked open the door to Room N-9, Becky's waiting and the bell's gonna ring any minute!

BECKY

I spent the first ten years of my teaching career as an LD, or Learning Disabilities teacher. Learning Disabilities comes under the umbrella of Special Education nomenclature. ED (Emotional Disabilities), CD (Cognitive Disabilities), etc., are all labels I'm sure you've heard. Labels can be so prejudiced. As soon as we hear the label, we have the tendency to box that person and shelve them as wild, dull, lazy, brilliant, etc. Use a label if it helps you better understand a student, but never truly assess them until you've really gotten to know them. I think most teachers understand this; we've had so many kids that just didn't fit the label.

As a side note, I guess I do have an exception. You see, my male teacher friends and I came up with a labeling system using clothing brand names to figuratively box ourselves and other teachers in. For example, my trendy teaching buddy who liked pressed clothes, expensive cologne, and found a wrinkle in fabric to be offensive was labeled "Versace." Another dear friend, who was neat, organized, and dependable, was labeled "Nautica." Being a struggling parent of four, I was allergic to an iron and found no problem wearing white socks with dark shoes, so I was labeled "St. John's Bay." Oh, here comes "Hilfiger" and "Ducks Unlimited," one too sophisticated and the other too into hunting for my taste. Okay, enough of *Project Runway–Label Edition*, let's get back to the kids.

As students, really, as human beings, we all have gifts and we all have handicaps when compared to everyone else. My job as a teacher was to find my students' gifts and help them use their strengths to succeed, to help prepare them for the workforce, but more importantly, to prepare them for life. That is a much bigger and nebulous set of criteria. Most teachers may hate labels, but for efficiency's sake and to get kids the help they need, the labels serve a purpose. They provide funding to give kids extra support that simply wouldn't be there without it. Once you're out of school, those school labels seem to fade away and you're judged more on how well you perform your job, not on an old classification. Certainly, the eternal labels of black and white, male and female, rich and poor, etc., will have to be dealt with in our society, but I've had many of my former LD students become great successes and a good share who have not, just like their "regular" and "gifted" classmates. How you use your gifts to overcome your handicaps, how hard and consistent you are willing to work, how well you get along with others—these are traits that a person needs to succeed in life. These are the attributes I tried to foster and instill in my students every day.

I've always had a soft spot when it came to kids who didn't seem to fit in or those who had a difficult time learning. I taught Special Education for a decade and Regular Education for twenty-one years. Whether in our society in general or in a school setting, the haves have always picked on the have-nots. I hated teasing and bullying as a teacher and tried to protect my kids as best I could. I think there'll be some video footage in my own teacher hell of me not noticing bullying in my classroom or hallway, or me not doing enough to stop it; but trust me, as teachers, we hate it. It hurts to see or know that one of your students is being bullied or picked on for whatever reason. We do all we can to empower kids on how to prevent, lessen, or stop bullying from happening, and we take the bullies to task. We know they are hurting as well, and they intimidate others to lessen their own pain and inadequacies. As teachers, we must love the unlovable.

One day, as I was looking out my classroom window onto the playground during lunch recess, I noticed a student of mine sitting all by herself on the edge of the sidewalk with a paperback in her hands. Hundreds of kids were running around her, laughing and playing tag. Others were in little groups, giggling and sharing stories. Some were on the grass playing touch football. But there she was, all alone, reading. It gave me pause to ponder. School was difficult for her, but she tried hard every day. At first glance, her teeth were over-sized, she was middle school awkward; she didn't wear the coolest clothes or know which songs topped the charts, and invariably some kids would make fun of her. This is the type of student I always tried to be extra kind to and give a little more attention. I wrote a poem about her. Of course, I've changed the name, but any two-syllable name will do. Becky, Jenny, Carly, you pick the name . .

there are plenty of them on any playground, at any recess, in any school, on any day of the year.

BECKY

Becky sits alone on the playground
And dreams about the friends she doesn't have.
Oh, she likes to read, about knights in shining armor
Movies starring heroes,
But the boys will notice braces more than smiles.
Becky sits alone in the classroom
And dreams about what she would like to be.
But learning's kind of hard, she'll never pass the bar
And her momma said, "Don't set your hopes too high."
Looks can be deceiving.
Strength comes from believing that
The only one who beats you is yourself.
Becky sits alone in the lunchroom
And tries to look away from nasty stares.
Middle school is cruel, where's the Golden Rule?
And she wonders if the world holds one who cares.
Looks can be deceiving
Strength comes from believing that
The only one who beats you is yourself
Becky sits alone on the playground
And notices that it's a beautiful day.
Sun shines warm and friendly, breezes blowing gently
Dry the single tear shed from her heart.

Every day, as teachers, we have an important task to accomplish in our classrooms. You won't find it in a list of objectives in a math or English teacher's edition. You won't be writing it on your whiteboard as a learning target, but look over that classroom of yours and find Becky. Find the one who looks the loneliest, the most forgotten, or the most noticed for all the wrong reasons. Give her or him your precious gift of time. Notice her. Tell her you need her to help you do something. Tell her with your words and smile that she is important and trusted. A few kind words and a smile can paint a rainbow in her soul that could last a lifetime.

Becky visited me in my classroom many years after I taught her. She had graduated college and was becoming very successful at her new job. She never knew I noticed her on the playground that one day so long ago, or that I wrote a poem about her, nor did she spot the smile in my heart that she had become a beautiful, competent, caring young adult.

WINNING IS NO MORE THAN THIS

I was the boys' cross country coach at my middle school for about twenty-five years. During those years there were a lot of bus rides, permission slip hassles, late nights waiting for students to get picked up, rainy meets, practices, scheduling emails, parental concerns, meet write-ups, etc. Since cross country was a non-cut sport, sometimes it felt more like a club than a sport. With excuses for missing meets and practices like haircut, dental, and doctor appointments, my dog had puppies, too much homework, got sick, "Jimmy made fun of me so I'm not coming," and of course, forgetting we had a meet, a serious coach can pull his or her hair out over the lack of commitment sometimes shown by the athletes.

On the other hand, there were always a handful of serious runners; athletes who were already itching for high school competition and who really wanted to succeed. As a cross country coach, I had my share of both serious competitors and those who were more interested in the bus rides with their friends. I always had the attitude that if you were out for middle school cross country, at least for those two to four hours, you weren't playing video games or watching TV. You were getting some exercise and learning a sport. You were getting stretches, working up a sweat, and tasting competition. Some runners who really joined the team for social reasons eventually became hard core competitors by the end of their three-year middle school cross country experience and went on to excel in high school.

Unlike football or basketball and most team sports, *everybody* competes in cross country. No one sits on the bench. While you may line up your team in the starting box with your fastest runners in the front, everyone else is right behind them, and they all take off together. It's what I love about the sport. Anyway, on to a favorite memory . .

For many years, we had a motto for our cross country team. It was even printed on the back of our team jerseys. The motto was derived from a poem by Dr. D. H. (Dee) Groberg, titled, "The Race." I first heard this poem while I was serving as a missionary in Tokyo, Japan a few years before I became a public school teacher. I was so impressed with this poem that I knew I wanted to use it with my cross country team and that it would be a great motivational tool for all the kids. Groberg's poem was actually made into a book and sold at motivational seminars throughout the country, it's that good. I won't mention the motto of our team until after the poem, but the first half goes like this, "Winning is no more than this . . " On the team, we would often go up to an athlete and say, "Winning is no more than this . . " and we would expect a rousing completion of the quote.

Well then. Without any further, adieu, here's the poem. Special thanks to Dr. Groberg, a man I greatly admire and respect, for his permission to use, "The Race."

THE RACE

I
"Quit! Give Up! You're beaten!"
They shout at me and plead.
"There's just too much against you now.
This time you can't succeed."
And as I start to hang my head
In front of failure's face,
My downward fall is broken
By the memory of a race.
And hope refills my weakened will

LARRY SHURILLA

As I recall that scene;
For just the thought of that short race
Rejuvenates my being.

II
A children's race; young boys, young men—
How I remember well.
Excitement, sure! But also fear;
It wasn't hard to tell.
They all lined up so full of hope
Each thought to win that race.
Or tie for first, or if not that,
At least take second place.
And fathers watched from off the side
Each cheering for his son.
And each boy hoped to show his dad
That he would be the one.
The whistle blew and off they went
Young hearts and hopes afire.
To win and be the hero there
Was each young boy's desire.
And one boy in particular
Whose dad was in the crowd
Was running near the lead and thought:
"My dad will be so proud!"
But as they speeded down the field
Across a shallow dip,
The little boy who thought to win
Lost his step and slipped.
Trying hard to catch himself
His hands flew out to brace,
And mid the laughter of the crowd

He fell flat on his face.
So down he fell and with him hope
—He couldn't win it now—
Embarrassed, sad, he only wished
To disappear somehow.
But as he fell his dad stood up
And showed his anxious face,
Which to the boy so clearly said,
"Get up and win the race!"
He quickly rose, no damage done,
—Behind a bit, that's all—
And ran with all his mind and might
To make up for his fall.
So anxious to restore himself
—To catch up and to win—
His mind went faster than his legs:
He slipped and fell again!
He wished then he had quit before
With only one disgrace.
"I'm hopeless as a runner now;
I shouldn't try to race."
But in the laughing crowd he searched
And found his father's face;
That steady look which said again:
"Get up and win the race!"
So up he jumped to try again
—Ten yards behind the last—
"If I'm to gain those yards," he thought,
"I've got to move real fast."
Exerting everything he had
He regained eight or ten,

LARRY SHURILLA

But trying so hard to catch the lead
He slipped and fell again!
Defeat! He lied there silently
—A tear dropped from his eye—
"There's no sense running anymore;
Three strikes! I'm out! Why try!"
The will to rise had disappeared;
All hope had fled away;
So far behind, So error prone;
A loser all the way.
"I've lost, so what's the use," he thought
"I'll live with my disgrace."
But then he thought about his dad
Who soon he'd have to face.
"Get up," an echo sounded low.
"Get up and take your place;
You were not meant for failure here.
Get up and win the race."
"With borrowed will get up," it said,
"You haven't lost at all.
"For winning is no more than this:
To rise each time you fall."
So up he rose to run once more,
And with a new commit
He resolved that win or lose
At least he wouldn't quit.
So far behind the others now,
—The most he'd ever been—
Still he gave it all he had
And ran as though to win.
Three times he'd fallen, stumbling;

Three times he rose again;
Too far behind to hope to win
He still ran to the end.
They cheered the other runner
As he crossed the line first place.
Head high, and proud, and happy;
No falling; no disgrace.
But when the fallen youngster
Crossed the line last place,
The crowd gave him the greater cheer,
For finishing the race.
And even though he came in last
With head bowed low, unproud,
You would have thought he won the race
To listen to the crowd.
And to his dad he sadly said,
"I didn't do too well."
"To me, you won," his father said.
"You rose each time you fell."

III
And now when things seem dark and hard
And difficult to face,
The memory of that little boy
Helps me in my race.
For all of life is like that race,
With ups and downs and all,
And all you have to do to win,
Is rise each time you fall.
"Quit! Give Up! You're Beaten!"
They still shout in my face.
But another voice within me says:

"GET UP AND WIN THE RACE!"

After reading the poem to the team, I would ask, "Who was the father in the poem?" A few hands would invariably go up and the kids would say things like their dad, mom, God, brother, sister, teacher, best friend, etc. I would respond they were all absolutely correct and remind them there will always be someone cheering them on. There will always be someone in their corner, accepting their mistakes and encouraging them to get up when failure hits and to keep on trying. If no one else, you've always got Coach Shurilla!

And now, reader, it's time for your pop quiz! You remember those, don't you? I bet you loved them, especially in math class. Well, here's your Coach Shurilla cross country quiz. If I happen to bump into you at the gas station or in a Walmart parking lot, will you be able to fill in the blanks?

Winning is no more than this: __ _____ _____ ____ ___ ____.

I knew you'd look back!

JACKPOT!

What is it with teachers and treats? Now, I guess this phenomenon is not solely restricted to schools; I would imagine similar things happening in small business offices throughout the United States, but since my expertise lies in the public education environment, permit me to continue gorging on glutton-rich, gastrointestinal gossip!

First of all, snacks comprising of candies, cupcakes, donuts, Danish Kringles (a Wisconsin favorite), potato chips, cookies, chocolate, etc., are ubiquitous in public schools. Treats are found in the main office, teachers' work room, guidance office, teacher's phone office, gym office, Home Economics' room, group areas, cafeteria, and don't forget, smack center on your desk! Now this is not an all-inclusive list, but suffice it to say, that it has cost the best blood of this generation to gather all this culinary recon-intelligence into one central location where it can be of most benefit to humanity—my mind, and ultimately, my stomach.

It has taken the better part of a teaching career to pool together this data in order to facilitate a more efficient use of my time for the proverbial "office run during my free period." Surely, you are familiar with the office run (and yes, I will call you Surely). You know, when you have time to run down to the office and check your mailbox? This run often takes place during your "free" period; the non-student-contact time you have after the office calls in your room reminding you of your IEP meeting in five minutes, or the time you have after the kids straggling behind in your classroom seeking attention or extra help on an assignment have been written their passes, or the minutes you have left after answering a hot-button email from a disgruntled parent .. you know, *that* free time!

Whatever time *is* left, you rendezvous with your fellow teacher battalion at the designated coordinates (usually a central hall location), haul-butt down to the office, avoid making eye contact with the secretaries so they won't ask you to sub and wipe away what's left of your prep period, check your mailbox, and if you're lucky, oh so very lucky, you might get a chance to crack open the time window for a potential jackpot run.

Ahh yes, a jackpot: the mother lode of baked goodness, the hidden treasure trove of tasty treats, the object and design of my existence. There might be a bowl of chewy caramels and premier chocolates put far away from the Jolly Rancher and peppermint bowls for special occasions, but where will it be found today? I've already listed a number of possible jackpot sites, but time and energy limit where you can check. While all these sites have proven successful at one time or another, seldom, if ever, have they yielded their bounty on the same day. Thus, the jackpot run, like any fishing trip, is filled with near misses, days when you get skunked, and the day of days when you cast your net and haul in a catch that will widen your inflatable waistline!

It's 1:36, the kids are restless to get to their next class, and it's about two minutes before our next office run. I heard the phys ed office had some donuts and a Gardetto's sighting was reported in the Family and Consumer Education room. Jackpot?!

LARRY SHURILLA

TROJANS! TROJANS! TROJANS!

When I began my teaching career, our middle school's mascot was the Trojan. I am not an expert on the history of the Trojan warrior, but I believe it has its roots in the Greek–Trojan war that pitted the great Achilles of Greece against the heroic Hector of Troy. Of course, the great battle was for the beautiful Helen of Troy, and ultimately the Trojan empire.

A Trojan warrior was fearless, strong, obedient, noble, and full of integrity: all great attributes for an aspiring middle schooler. Apparently during the late 1960s, when our middle school was built, it was a fine and popular name for a school mascot. Nowadays, whenever I hear the word "Trojan" I immediately think of Brad Pitt fighting Eric Bana in the movie *Troy*, or I may think of the collegiate football team, the USC Trojans, or I may think of a latex device that shall not be named in a public school setting. Well, it's not *supposed* to be mentioned, unless you're in Human Growth and Development class.

During the initial years of my teaching career in the mid-1980s, the first image that came to mind upon hearing the name of our mascot was the fierce warrior. As time wore on, however, the rumblings of a snicker or two could occasionally be heard after somebody said "Trojan." Ultimately, for me, the death of our mascot came on a beautiful spring day at track and field practice.

Our head coach, a barrel-chested, fun-loving, behemoth of a man, was overseeing the usual warm-up exercises on the grass field next to our school. In order to infuse some excitement into an otherwise lackluster warm-up with the kids simply going through the motions, Coach B. grabbed the proverbial Trojan by the bristle-feathered helmet and shouted, "Okay! Everyone line up here. We're gonna put our arms up in the air, wave our hands back and forth, and while we're doing our high-knees warm-up jogging downfield, spin around and shout out, 'Trojans! Trojans! Trojans!' Like this!"

Coach B. then modeled the perfect, spinning, hand-shaking warrior, shouting, "Trojans! Trojans! Trojans!" to the delight of all the assistant coaches and students. The athletes, ever ready and obedient, lined up quickly like a regimented attack force and on Coach B.'s cue, they began their twirling jog and shouted with a cry that could've crumbled the walls of Troy, "Condoms! Condoms! Condoms!"

For me, that was the symbolic end to the Trojan Warrior mascot, a dagger to the heart—or in this case, an arrow to the heel—of a once noble warrior. A year or two later, the student council held a school-wide vote to determine the new mascot. I only remember two of the choices on the list, the ultimate winner and the old standby Trojans. And so, you may ask, what is the new mascot voted in by the democratic process of popular opinion? The Bulldogs.

Besides determination, I fail to see the virtues of such a symbol. When I think of a bulldog, I picture a salivating pygmy with a crumpled Sherpa coat, squatting in my backyard doing the unimaginable. This is our mascot?! This is the symbol of our student body and the icon which will inspire and motivate us to greater achievements? I think not! Perhaps our new cheer on the sidelines of basketball games should be, "Drown in drool, fool! Drown in drool!"

So we have come to the end of a once proud era. A noble Trojan warrior is bested by the sharp blade of twirling sexual innuendo and all that is left of our once proud heritage is a leather skirted Brad Pitt and the USC marching band at halftime. Gooooooooo Bulldogs?!

WHEN THE HAND GOES UP

As teachers, we've been taught that a good technique to use when beginning almost any introductory lesson is to elicit responses from the students. This allows us to gauge their depth of background knowledge on any given topic as well as engage their minds and focus their attention away from the cute girls sitting next to them or the buzzing cell phones in their pockets. Calling on students to share their thoughts is also a good way to break up their morning nap in math class. In any event, once a question is asked by the teacher, hands will invariably go up.

It was one of those days when our regular teaching schedule was greatly disturbed due to a school assembly, testing, or whatever, so we planned a goal-setting activity. We opened up the moveable wall between two of our classrooms and gathered about a hundred of our kids together into a large group setting. Since this gathering was early in the school year, we thought it was a good time for the students to brainstorm and set an achievable goal for the first quarter of the year.

On this particular day, I was leading the introductory discussion and I recall making a few brief remarks about how a goal should be realistic and something they really want to achieve, not something that they're doing to please someone else. As we were finishing off the discussion, to help those who were having trouble coming up with ideas, I asked for volunteers to share their goals and what they were thinking about. Then the hands went up!

The first student called upon shared that she was going to make better use of her assignment notebook, that this would help her stay organized and know what the homework assignments were when she got home, etc. We were all nodding in agreement. Good goal! An organized assignment notebook is a good idea and it helps many students stay on track and know what is expected of them on a daily basis.

The next hand went up and a sixth-grade boy said his goal was to keep his locker clean and organized. He said his locker was usually a mess and this made finding anything crazy difficult; those few minutes spent digging through rubble would often make him late for class and he'd get a tardy slip. We all agreed and said that was a worthy goal and an organized locker would increase efficiency and ability to move to classes on time and be better prepared. Good goal!

Finally, amid what looked like a bamboo forest of arms and hands waving in the air, I called on one. I said something like "Okay, Bridget, what's your goal going to be?" Bridget responded, "I want to walk."

Her response hit me with a thud and all preprogrammed teacher thinking came to a screeching halt. After a momentary pause, I was reminded that Bridget was wheelchair bound, that a debilitating disease had weakened her legs and taken from her the gift of independent walking mobility. In those brief moments after her response, as my mind spun,

I pictured her with her Special Education teachers, walking down the hallways of our school with a mechanical contraption that allowed her to be upright with the aid of straps, and slowly drag with gargantuan effort, those heavy, numb legs, one at a time, one in front of the other, painstakingly slow, yet with determined progress.

After the initial knockdown blow, my mind got up off the mat and I responded, "Yes, Bridget, being able to walk is an excellent goal. And with the incredible effort you've shown so far, I don't doubt you'll achieve your goal one day!" She smiled and went busily back to her goal-setting paper, eagerly drawing and writing.

Hope. Besides love, is there a more important word in all of human language? When students feel hope, they work. When students feel hope, they dream. When students have hope, they achieve and are happy. Our schools and classes are filled with the hopeless, those who have been beaten down by poverty, handicaps, and dysfunctional families. One of our jobs as teachers is to instill hope in the hopeless; to help a child see the strengths they possess and their uniqueness in the world and how their uniqueness is beautiful and makes them one of a kind.

I have a favorite quote from *Star Trek* I've used many times over the years when discussing this topic of uniqueness. Oftentimes, a student can feel lost in the crowd, like they are the offspring of the Invisible Man, or just another dumb kid. Sixth graders walking down those big terrazzo hallways, seemingly swimming upstream against a school of hostile eighth grade piranhas, can feel so small and inconsequential. Enter the good doctor, Dr. Leonard McCoy, "Bones," from *Star Trek*.

In one particular episode, when Captain Kirk was feeling especially burdened and inadequate in executing his role as Captain of the USS Enterprise, Dr. McCoy offered this starry gem of encouragement:

"In this galaxy, there's a mathematical probability of three million Earth-type planets. And in all of the universe, three million, million galaxies like this. And in all of that . . . and perhaps more, only one of each of us. [*pause*] Don't destroy the one named Kirk."

Thanks, Bones, I needed that. But how true it is! Instead of feeling dwarfed and insignificant by the immensity of space, let us focus on the absolute reality of our uniqueness in the universe. There is no one else quite like us. There is only one you. There is only one Bridget. The bigger the school, the town, the city, the more unique we become. Don't feel like just another lump of coal in a grill; feel like a diamond in the rough! Feel like the success you were meant to be! As teachers, we have the unbelievably awesome opportunity to be the igniters of hope in our students. We can be the ones who make a difference in our students' lives. We can love them unconditionally, and help them work through their doubts, inadequacies, handicaps, and fears. We must never give up on them and always be an example of a competent, caring adult. Show them why they, personally, can hope for a great future.

For a number of years, as we held our open house for new sixth graders and their parents a few days before school began, I would often begin the evening with a slide of Neil Armstrong and the Wright Brothers and ask the kids if they knew who these fellows were? Invariably, someone would get it Wright . . I mean correct. I would continue talking about how I was watching the *NBC Evening News* one night and Brian Williams began a segment espousing that there were no more Neil Armstrongs, that the day of exploration and true American hero boundary breakers was over. I couldn't have disagreed with him more and I like Brian Williams. I told the parents that as teachers we see Neil Armstrongs and Wright Brothers and Christa McAuliffes and Madame Curies in our classes every year. And it's true. The age of exploration has only just begun and with the greatest learning tools in the history of the world at our disposal, the greatest achievements in history are near as well.

Find a talent in each of your students. Use that talent or ability as the wedge of hope in that child's life. Let them see their personal potential through your seasoned eyes. Reward each success with a morsel of your time and help the awkward build their resiliency.

Every day is an adventure in the public school classroom. You can never be sure what those crazy kids are going to say or do next. So, when you're walking through a new topic of study with your class, although you can never truly be sure what to expect when that hand goes up, give Neil, Orville, Christa, and Bridget a chance to open up and shine. There's only one like each of them, and you, in this whole universe!

ROOM N9

IF GOD WERE HERE RIGHT NOW

In the public school setting, references to God surprisingly do come up quite often. Kids talk about their midweek religion classes or where they went to church over the weekend or the church camp they just attended. Occasionally you may find a student praying at lunch or even offering a silent prayer in class for help on a test. I felt my role as a public school educator was not to use my influence to push any religious agenda, while at the same time allowing the full, free exercise of my students' religious beliefs.

Parents and students have given me anti-evolution DVDs, religious Christmas cards, prayer cards, religious-themed popcorn canisters, emails, and voice messages, etc. All are welcome and represent the free exercise of their religious views and help me to get to know their kids (my students) better. Religious beliefs can be a great motivator to a child and as a teacher I am looking for anything that can help my students succeed. A belief in God can help students overcome their inadequacies. It can be a core influence on a child. Just because you're a public school teacher, don't be afraid to reference a child's belief system in order to help them. This is definitely a hot button topic in education, but use your professional judgement and don't fear religion; use it to help those students who believe it.

I remember my first year of teaching: 1985. Before there was a computer in every classroom and fifty emails a day, we would receive many little notes each day from the office in our mailboxes. Just imagine if all your emails were printed out daily and placed in your office mailbox! What a propagating pile of disposable desk doo-doo that would soon become. Well, that's the way it was, smart phone people, and we liked it! Okay, we didn't like it. In any era, no news is good news, right?

Anyway, one day I received a little note saying my principal wanted to meet with me. "Curious," I thought, "Why does the principal want to see me?" My mind quickly raced through all the likely suspects: Jimmy's mom is mad because he's failing science; Christy's dad thinks I give too much homework; Abby's parents think I don't give *enough* homework; Billy said I made him cry . . you know the rap sheet.

Nothing really stood out in my mind as I entered the principal's office. I really didn't know what I was getting into. "Have a seat, Larry," the principal invited, as he gestured toward the soft plushy chair that had swallowed up many a non-compliant teacher or disruptive student in the past.

As I sank into the bottomless chair (think of the movie *Get Out*), I had just enough time to hoarsely say, "Thanks, Mr. H. What's going on?"

"Well, Larry," Mr. H. parlayed, "It seems you've been using school time for religious purposes. Is that true?"

"What do you mean, Mr. H.?"

"One of the staff said they saw you reading the Bible in your classroom. Is this true?"

"Yes, Mr. H., that is true. I try to read a little bit from the Bible every morning during my prep period first hour. I believe it helps center me and makes me a better teacher."

"That may be true, Larry, but in a public school, it's probably not a good idea. Do your studies at home."

After I pulled the grappling hook and nylon ladder out of my backpack, I climbed out of the chair and left the principal's office feeling betrayed. I was narced on by a fellow teacher! I thought a preparation period was just that—a preparation for teaching period. If I felt reading a few scriptures in the privacy of my classroom before any students arrived was a good way to prepare for the rigors of the teaching day, who was he or she to judge that as inappropriate?

In the end, it wasn't that big of a deal. I still read scriptures to begin each day, just at home before I got to school. But here is another confession! For all thirty-one years of my teaching career, I had a 5x7 postcard on my desk of Jesus with children gathered around him and one sitting on his lap. No one ever complained to the principal about it. Occasionally, a student or fellow teacher would notice it, but when you think that picture was on my desk for thirty-one years, you would've thought I would've been asked about it a lot! Not so, my teaching friend, not so. I guess people are just a little too afraid of getting into weird faith discussions to broach the topic, and that is just fine. If that picture gave me a little help, a little more patience, a little more forgiveness—and it did—then it served its purpose well.

"But Jesus said, 'Suffer little children, and forbid them not, to come unto me: for of such is the kingdom of heaven.'" (Matthew 19:14)

I've always loved that scripture and see in the eyes of children something of the divine; a purity, a guilelessness, and gentleness that too often gets erased—or perhaps a better term would be *buried*—as we grow up.

About ten years into my career, I made the switch from Learning Disabilities to Regular Education teacher. As a Regular Education teacher, I was able to have more direct instruction with larger bodies of students, which was something I sought after.

One day, during one of those first years in regular ed., I happened to be with a small group of students who had been left behind from a large group activity to make up some missing homework assignments. One of the students was busy working on an assignment at his desk, when out of the blue he asked me, "Hey, Mr. Shurilla! If God were here right now, what would you say to him?"

Wow! This is one of those questions and moments that don't come along too often in public school! It was a question I had never prepared for or ever anticipated answering. I paused and repeated his question to buy me a little time to think .. and pray. "You know, if God were right here right now, I think I would say to Him .. 'I love you.' And you know what I wish he'd say to me?"

"No, Mr. S. What?"

"Welcome home."

RAMBO

This next memory always surprises me for its simplicity, brevity, and how others seem to make such a big deal out of it.

Let me begin by saying 1985 or '86 must have been a simpler time. A time featuring Billy Crystal on *Saturday Night Live*, Tommy Hilfilger Menswear, *Cheers*, and *Back to the Future* with Marty McFly topping the box office. I don't think I would've done this today. The school climate has changed, especially how we are perceived by the public and this "performance" would probably not be well received.

I'm a prankster. I love to have fun with my fellow workers and break the locked-in teacher mindset so many of them exhibit the moment they enter the school. You've seen it! A seemingly happy, bubbly, lighthearted teacher, upon entering the school's black cast iron gates, becomes a distracted, incoherent phrase-muttering prairie dog, intent on being the first to get to their classroom to go over and over and over, those daily lesson plans before the students stampede into their classroom! Let's just say I loved to break things up a bit in the sometimes stuffy atmosphere of many a school. So, here's the prank . .

I believe it was my second year of teaching—I never would have dreamed of doing this my first year. I must've been watching one of the *Rambo* movies starring Sylvester Stallone, and I got it into my head that hiding in a teachers' workroom with all the lights off, waiting for an unsuspecting teacher to open the door to turn the lights on, and then popping out from behind a cabinet and shouting something would be a great prank! Harmless, right? I don't see why some folks would make such a fuss about this! People get surprised all the time, don't they? Well, I did leave out the fact I was wearing a red bandanna across my forehead and wielding a thin red pole like a machete. A guy jumping out, red bandanna-clad, slashing a red stick, and grunting when the lights go on . . what's the big deal? All right, there is still one more fact that I failed to mention and maybe this is what gets everybody's undies in a bundle; I was shirtless.

Rambo never wore a shirt and if I was going to be imitating him, for reality's sake, I had to take mine off. So, there it is. I was hiding in a dark teacher workroom, holding my red "machete," had my bandanna on to drink up the tropical jungle sweat pouring down my face, shirtless, and ready to let out a macho cry of attack.

All went as planned. A new female teacher, who came unsuspectingly looking for a cup of coffee or a quick call to an angry parent, approached the door, turned the key, and as she flipped on the light, out I jumped, roaring like a Klingon at a mating ritual and crisscrossing my machete like Napoleon Dynamite's nun chucks!

For some odd reason, this teacher startled a bit, laughed, shook her head, mumbled something about an idiot, and left the room. I quickly put my shirt back on, took my bandanna off, placed the machete in the corner and returned to my room to get ready for sixth-hour science. That's the whole story. No student ever saw Rambo and only one teacher did, but for some odd reason, the word got out and people loved to hear the "Rambo Story." I guess I better keep my shirtless appearances to cutting the front lawn, chest waxing, or body surfing. Was the prank worth the risk? Well, for one brief moment in that preoccupied prairie dog's day, she forgot about the pressures of school when encountering a crazed John Rambo in a dark, steamy workroom. I guess it was worth it .. for me anyway.

THE HEART OF A CHAMPION

In our sixth grade classes, we used to show a clip from the movie *Chariots of Fire* to our kids most every year. In the clip, we see Eric Liddell, a runner from Scotland, get tripped and fall down during a 400-meter race on a grass track. As Eric shakes off the effects of the fall, he sees the other runners speedily slipping away from him. He then musters a determined grimace and proceeds to get up, slowly catch, and ultimately overtake the field to win the race! The effort had its price, as Eric lay gasping and almost hyperventilating on the track. That look of determination, that focused willpower, is what I concentrated on and talked about whenever we showed that clip to the kids. As a wise man once said, "If the desire is strong enough, the performance is assured."

Later in the movie, Eric states, "And where does this power come from? It comes from within." The following story is—in a manner of speaking—my story of an Eric Liddell. It's the story of a middle schooler who wouldn't let anything or anyone get in his way, a middle schooler with the heart of a champion.

The old adage, "Be careful what you say, someone may be listening" was never truer than in the case of Steven. Perhaps you've taught a student or coached an athlete like Steven—the kind of kid that has an unshakably positive attitude and is oblivious to the concept of failure, even when he's failing. He's the kind of kid that actually does everything you ask of him and it works. Well, here's the story of a kid like that, a true story of success and what it takes to become the best.

You've already read about our team motto: "Winning is no more than this: to rise each time you fall!" A number of years ago I coached an athlete that embodied the essence of our motto. Steven joined our cross country team as a typical sixth grade boy, a kid who looked more accustomed to playing computer games than running competitively. He was not someone you watch run and say, "Now here's a future champ!" And I've had those types of athletes. I remember a girl who, in her first race, was so far ahead of all the other sixth and seventh grade girls, and due to her inexperience, took a wrong turn on the cross country course, got lost, took some time to get back on track, and still won the race! As a sixth grader, *that* is impressive. Steven did not have that kind of ability . . or at least, I didn't think he did.

Whenever we ran our warmups or workouts, Steven would be the last one to finish and at a good distance behind all the rest. When you'd watch him run, you'd expect him to be discouraged or depressed at being so far behind everyone else. Believe me, I've had a ton of athletes who were in Steven's position, who would quit or moan and say, "What's the use? I suck at running. I'm quitting."

Of course, we coaches would respond, "Don't give up! You're just a sixth grader! Give your body time to grow and develop. We promise you, if you keep trying, you will get better! You may not win blue ribbons, but you will get better and see your times go down. Just don't give up! Don't quit! Keep at it a little longer!" How many times have we said things like that? They usually fall on deaf ears, right? But not always. Steven was an Arizona sunbaked, dehydrated sponge for positive affirmations. There was no positive quote too short or too long for Steven to grasp and make his own:

"Don't give up, Steven!"

"I won't give up, Coach!"

"Keep trying, Steven!"

"I'll keep trying, Coach!

"You're working hard, Steven!"

"I'm working hard, Coach!"

"Winning is no more than this, Steven!"

"To rise each time you fall, Coach!"

Steven's attitude was his greatest asset. Nothing could get him down. He drank in all the coaching affirmations and always looked ahead to the next practice, the next workout, the next race.

The first couple of races, Steven took dead last, and when you have hundreds of middle schoolers running these cross country races, last is saying something. But Steven's attitude was apparent. "I'm getting better, Coach. I was only two yards behind Tommy this time. I'm feeling stronger and stronger each race!" Steven could always find something positive about every race or practice. He focused on what he was doing well and kept trying to stretch better, run practices better, and compete better at the invitationals.

Slowly, almost unperceptively, Steven began to improve. By the end of his sixth grade season, Steven was no longer the last finisher in various runs and drills at our practices. He also started to come in front of a runner or two on our team and would beat about ten or fifteen runners at the big cross country invitationals. And Steven would let you know about it.

"I beat Jimmy and Connor this time, Coach! I beat those two guys from Falls Middle School today, Coach! They beat me two weeks ago, but I got them today!"

Steven had begun to taste success and he liked it. He liked it a lot. He had listened to everything his coaches had been saying and saw himself improve. That is truly the main thing I like about sports: the ability to see growth in yourself after applying consistent effort. You can change yourself and become what you want to become. Just never give up and never lose sight of your goals. Steven was on his way.

As coaches, we always told our athletes to stay active and run over the summer. "Don't wait until the first cross country practice in the fall to start getting in shape," we would tell them. "Run with your dad or brother or sister or friends over the summer and you'll come to cross country in September ready to take off and compete!" These words usually fell victim to Northern Wisconsin vacations, sunny days at the pool or beach, or the green-eyed Xbox monster. In any case, Steven was not your average middle schooler. Steven really listened to his coaches and applied his lessons.

At the beginning of Steven's seventh grade season, he came up to me and told me he had been running all summer long with his brother and couldn't wait for the season to begin. I thought in the back of my head, "He actually did what we told him to do?! Could Steven really turn out to be a decent runner?" I dismissed the thought. "He's just too far behind the others, physically, to really be able to compete."

Steven's attitude remained one of ultimate optimism and perseverance. He was no longer the guy everyone waited for to finish his workout or race. Steven was right in the middle of the pack of our seventh grade runners and was also in the middle of the pack at our cross country meets. Now, when you're competing against a field of 300 runners, getting 150th place is a glass half empty or a glass half full scenario. To the pessimist, you got beat by 149 runners. "I suck! This sport is *not* for me!"

On the other hand, to the optimist, getting 150th place out of a field of 300 means that you beat 150 runners. "I just beat 150 kids my same age from all around Wisconsin. I wonder if I keep working hard if I can crack into the top hundred next time." This was the attitude of Steven. His glass was always half full and the way he was looking at it, his water was bubbling up and nothing could stop the ascent.

In eighth grade, by the end of the season, Steven eventually became our No. 1 runner! All those racers' backs he was looking at for three years were now looking at his! He was competing at the highest level in middle school cross country and was winning Top Ten ribbons. But his success didn't stop there. Steven moved on to high school, and in his senior year became the male cross country champion of his conference. Following Steven's great example, his senior high school team won the first team conference cross country championship in school history!

Steven went on to compete at the college level and was in his university's top five runners. After college, Steven eventually returned to his high school to coach cross country and track. While coaching cross country at his old school, they won two more conference titles and Steven coached the first state qualifying team in forty years as well! Steven's infectiously positive attitude not only contributed to his personal success, it rubbed off on the youngsters he now coaches and will coach for years to come.

"I keep getting better, Coach!"

"Yes you do, Steven! And so do those fortunate athletes under your care."

Ultimately, as Eric Liddell taught us by winning the 1924, 400-meter dash at the Summer Olympics in Paris, the power to win comes from within. But it can *begin* from without. It can begin with that one encouraging word from a parent or friend or coach that says, "I think you have some talent here. Wow, you have really shown a big improvement since the last time I saw you. Do you see how far you have come since last year?" There is great power in the application of justified praise. Find something in the athlete or student that deserves recognition and lavish it on. Just remember it can't be fake praise. You need to catch them doing something worthwhile and if you look hard enough, you will surely find it. Remember, all it takes is a single spark to ignite an inferno.

I know I've learned my lesson. I really do believe in the power of positive thinking and believing in yourself. When I see a kid at the end of the pack now, I don't think, "Well, that kid should give it up and try something else." Rather, I remember Steven was once a runner like that, straggling behind out there, and he became a champion. What kind of heart beats in that kid out there? Could he or she be the next Olympic champion? Do I hear Vangelis' theme song from *Chariots of Fire* playing?

You bet I do!

UNCLE LARRY

As teachers, we get called lots of names. Many of which I cannot print, but those are usually shouted in outbursts when a student has really lost it. You'll only hear them once in a blue moon.

Day to day, I usually heard "Mr. Shurilla, Mr. S., or Coach," in all my years of teaching, but every once in a while, a kid would get ahold of your first name. Now, I do understand there are a few teachers that don't mind it and actually prefer to have their students address them by their first name, but I always thought I needed that wall of professionalism that a Mr. or Mrs. Something provided. I didn't want to get too chummy with the kids, and hearing a "Hey, Larry!" from a kid in the back of the classroom was as bad as scratching your fingernails on a chalkboard or chewing on aluminum foil. Give me Liberty, Death, or Mr. S., but don't you *dare* call me Larry!

Somewhere in the middle of my career, I had the fortune of teaching three inseparable girls. Let's call them Ally, Bella, and Kate. They were always together in class, at lunch, in the halls, by their lockers. They were also very bright and fun-loving. They would get the giggles at almost anything and were so good-natured that you just couldn't get mad at them. They would get the jokes your other kids wouldn't and they were kind to everyone.

As luck would have it, one day some teacher must've been talking to me by my desk and said something like, "So Larry, when are you gonna get to mixed numbers in math?" Bing! Bing! Bong! The ears on Ally shot up like a cat when you shake a Friskies' box, and she said with a crazed look of delight shining in her eyes, "Mr. S., your name is Larry?!"

"Well, what am I going to say now?" I thought. She heard it. I'm not going to lie about my name, so I said, "Yeah, Ally, that's my first name."

Mistake. I should've lied. The name spread between the three faster than a viral cat video on YouTube and they kept using it. It was "Larry this" and "Larry that" until finally, I had to get serious with them. "Now look girls, you can't keep calling me, Larry. We have to keep things a bit more professional in a school setting. That's just how it is."

They huddled up for a moment and then one of them, staring at me with big eyes like the cat from *Shrek* said, "Can we call you, *Uncle* Larry, then?"

This book is about confessions, successes, and mistakes, right? Mistake number two. I just couldn't say no. So I said, "Okay, you can call me Uncle Larry, but only if other kids aren't around and only once in a while, okay?"

Needless to say, the girls were ecstatic and after about two microseconds, I realized that this could go south really fast. Imagine me teaching

29

something in class, and the principal drops in for an observation, and Bella or Kate goes, "Uncle Larry, do we have to do the evens or the odd problems for homework?"

The principal turns her head toward me and mumbles, "Uncle Larry? A bit informal aren't we, *Mister* Shurilla? Why don't you come down to my office after class and we'll have a little chat with the HR director."

Well, luckily, something like that never happened. The girls were true to their word and only occasionally would I hear the two sacred words pronounced. I can still picture Kate, waiting at the classroom door until all the other students had left and whispering, "Bye, Uncle Larry," and then scooting out the door to meet up with her friends for lunch.

Time marches on. If you think it doesn't, just try backing it up one second. You may wish it would go faster, but it never slows down, stops, or goes into reverse. Time relentlessly moves forward and no power yet invented can change that. Whether you're having a good year and you want to teach that class forever or you've got a group of Satan's spawn and can't wait to bless the seventh grade teachers with the "Children of the Corn," you only have them for one year and they move on to the next grade.

When you teach for more than thirty years an awful lot of things can happen to those kids. Some good. Some bad. And all the kids grow up. You see your students move on to seventh and eighth grade and then on to high school. You may see a picture of them in the district newsletter, run into them at the grocery store, or hear about their accomplishments from their parents or siblings, but nothing can prepare you for the moment when you hear that one of your former kids is going to die.

Cancer does its deadly drop-ins to households indiscriminately. There are no protections on the homes of the young and innocent. One day, about four years after we taught her, we heard Kate was dying of cancer. Time was a blur after we were informed and suddenly Kate had passed. The funeral was set, and we, a group of her old sixth grade teachers, went to the church to pay our final respects. The death of one so young, so full of life, seemed insidious. She was in the bloom of life and had so much to look forward to.

There was a long line of friends and loved ones that weekday evening at the church. Kate had touched many people in the community and everyone there wanted to show they cared. As I looked around the church at all the friendly people quietly talking to each other, the beautiful flowers, the family gathered around the casket, I couldn't help thinking this shouldn't be happening. We should be here for Kate's wedding, not a funeral. But I also felt an unmistakable feeling of love and gratitude that though her life was short, it was filled with love.

Soon we were shaking hands with Kate's parents and expressing our sympathies when we spied Ally and Bella near the end of the family line. As we drew close, we formed a group hug, the old sixth grade teachers and our two former students. I don't recall exactly what we said, but it wasn't much, just that we cared. We held onto each other for a moment or two longer and then Ally squeaked out two of the sweetest words I have ever heard in my life. With tears in her eyes and a smile on her face, she quickly whispered, "Uncle Larry."

LIVE LONG AND PROSPER

"A life is like a garden. Perfect moments can be had, but not preserved, except in memory. LLAP."

This was the final tweet from the actor Leonard Nimoy, better known as television's Mr. Spock from *Star Trek*. The quote is also quite representative of teaching. This book is like my garden and the flowers are my teaching memories, preserved for anyone inclined to check them out. If you ask any of my students what my favorite television program of all time is, you'll get a resounding "*Star Trek*" for an answer.

As a seven-year-old boy, there I was that Thursday night in September of 1966 at seven o'clock, eyes glued to Channel 4 on the TV, for the very first episode of *Star Trek*. My brothers and I were sci-fi fanatics. We watched *Lost in Space, The Outer Limits, Voyage to the Bottom of the Sea*, and any cheap space movie we could tune our three channels to. *Star Trek*—with its phasers, star ships, communicators, tricorders, transporters, and photon torpedoes—looked to be a potent cocktail for any thirsty sci-fi fan . . and it did not disappoint. We absolutely loved it and haven't stopped loving it for over fifty years.

With about six years left in my teaching career, I thought it was time to try something new at our middle school. I decided to organize a Science Fiction Club. I don't believe I ever heard of any other middle school having a sci-fi club before, but having had so many conversations with kids about sci-fi topics in my classroom, I knew there was a niche for this sort of thing.

I talked to the associate principal in charge of clubs and he agreed this club just might work. I got to work and made a few morning announcements plugging the club with talk of *Star Trek, Star Wars,* and classic sci-fi movies like *Forbidden Planet* and *This Island Earth.*

I believe we started out with about six or seven members. By the fifth year we had about twenty-five with a good mix of boys and girls! I structured the club with a fair chunk of time for discussion about any sci-fi topic the kids were interested in followed by time to play a card game called *Star Trek Uno,* and then on to the viewing of classic *Star Trek* TV episodes and timeless sci-fi movies.

My main goals as club advisor were to: give kids opportunities to make friends with others who had the same interests, give them an outlet for group discussions about things they loved, and ultimately give them a little more sense of belonging in the middle school, which can be a pretty frightening place when you're in the tween years. It was also my job to share with the kids my personal history and knowledge of sci-fi. Then they could use that as a base to see how sci-fi has evolved and morphed over the years.

I must say, the club was a lot of fun. We had some very heated discussions. Which was the best *Star Wars'* movie? What's better—*Star Trek* or *Star Wars*? Who is the best *Dr. Who*? What other plots exist in the *Star Wars* and *Star Trek* universe of books, games, and online websites? Who is the best *Star Trek* captain? Ahem, Kirk, of course!

Being a science teacher, my love of *Star Trek* was also useful in the classroom. How could a discussion of technological progress in the world not include *Star Trek* and its vision of the future? Desktop computers, view screens, and cordless communicators were all present in fiction before they were in reality. *Star Trek*'s harmonious blend of races working together, without prejudice and stereotyping, toward a common goal was also a fine projection of what the future could become. It's as important now as it was in the 1960s. I always told the kids in my science classes, "If we can think of it, we can create it! The world needs dreamers and doers who work together to better our world. Whether we've made the problem ourselves—like what to do with nuclear waste and plastic in the oceans—or the problem has existed for centuries—like cancer or how to achieve sustainable powered flight—there is no problem we cannot overcome with persistent effort, use of the technology of the day, and vision."

We're often told as educators that we need to keep the minds of our children open, flexible, and trained with problem-solving skills. Appropriate science fiction naturally leads our kids into these areas of the mind. We often get so caught up with the latest teaching technique fad that we lose sight of the most important component of teaching: motivation! If you have it, you can accomplish anything, and without it, you will accomplish nothing. Kids can be lazy or overwhelmed. Kids can be unable or unchallenged. These are some of the problems teachers face every day with kids in the same classroom trying to learn the same material. I have no magic solution here, but I will repeat, if you have a motivated student, you can accomplish anything and if you have an unmotivated student, you will accomplish nothing. Let us work on how to better motivate students by providing a safe and interesting classroom environment. I have also found that bringing science fiction into the classroom can help motivate many of our students.

Having taught for thirty-one years, I get the great pendulum of education. How certain disciplinary techniques, philosophies, and teaching pedagogies come into fashion and then, not too many years later, are branded as the worst methodology in history . . until the pendulum swings back and we do it all over again. I am reminded of Heidi Klum on *Project Runway*, a competitive fashion designing television show, and what she says each week to her fashion designers. "One week you are in, and the next, you are out!" And so it seems to be in education. One week, Robert Marzano, you are in, and the next week, Madeline Cheek Hunter, you are out! This swinging pendulum may be why we see more experienced teachers become so rigid in their unwillingness to change; because they've already been through multiple teaching fads and just want to rely on what has truly worked for them in their classrooms. Perhaps an attitude of, "keep the best, throw out the rest" may prove the most beneficial to teachers of all ages and experience levels.

If you're a science teacher, try bringing a little science fiction into your classroom and see if it doesn't amp up the motivation for a lot of your students. A two-minute movie clip showing a star ship extinguishing an active volcano with a cold fusion detonator is a great way to introduce a science lesson on volcanology. It may not be included in a Smartboard lesson plan or textbook, but it may motivate a majority of your students to actually listen to what you're talking about!

Finally, here's an unexpected bonus to bringing sci-fi into the classroom. One of the most creative homemade cards given to me for retirement by one of my students read as follows:

(ON THE COVER)

What's the
best way to say
Goodbye
and happy retirement
to your favorite
Science
teacher?

(NEXT PAGE)

To Infinity and
beyond!

*No that's Buzz
Lightyear.*

May the Force
be with

yo-

No, still doesn't sound right.

(NEXT PAGE)

Larry, I am your fath-

No, I'm not your father and that's still not it.

I've got it . . .

(LAST PAGE)

Live Long
and
Prosper!
From: Your Awesome Student

Now that's boldly going where no student has gone before! Truly, this card was a formative assessment indicating this student has been well taught in the annals of the purest science fiction.

A few days ago, I saw a T-shirt of a Peanuts' cartoon with Charlie Brown, head bowed down in depression, and Violet standing a step or two behind him. The bubble caption read, "I still miss Leonard Nimoy." My feelings exactly. Even the most magnificent of flowers seem only to last a moment in time, but therein lies part of their magic. That moment is so alive, so precious, and may live on in our memories forever.

LLAP, my old friend.

ROOM N9

FIDDLING ABOUT

In the late 1970s, I was an Elton John fanatic (still am) and I was very excited to hear that Elton would be making a movie appearance in The Who's rock opera, *Tommy*. Elton assumed the role of The Pinball Wizard and played his keyboard-mounted pinball machine with utter delight as he sang, "That deaf, dumb, and blind kid sure plays a mean pinball!" In the movie, there was a rather disturbing scene with Wicked Uncle Ernie, played by The Who's drummer, Keith Moon. It was alluded to in the movie that Wicked Uncle Ernie may have abused the handicapped Tommy by, as the song goes, "Fiddling about, fiddling about, fiddling about!"

Which brings me to something I witnessed once many years ago at the middle school. No, it wasn't any kind of molestation, but as you will soon learn, it was "fiddling about" and it was disturbing.

I was walking down the sixth-grade hall near the end of the school day, returning to my classroom during a prep period, when a female Learning Disabilities teacher stopped me for a moment and said, "Larry, can you go into the boys' bathroom for a minute and see what's taking Jake so long or if he's having some sort of problem? Maybe he's not in there and is wandering the halls somewhere? I sent him to the bathroom about twenty minutes ago and he's still not back."

"Sure, I'll check it out," I said, naively. I had absolutely no idea what I was about to witness. As I pushed open the creaky wooden door and walked past a tiled divider, there I saw Jake, buck naked, fiddling with his privates and skipping up and down across the far wall of the bathroom. Being the great detective and psychologist that I am, I shouted out, "Jake! What are you doing? Why aren't you dressed?"

Jake stopped dead in his tracks with confusion on his face, looked at his hands, and said, "I was hot, so I took my clothes off."

"Well, put your clothes back on and get back to class fast! Your teacher is wondering what took you so long and is waiting for you in the hall!"

I went back into the hall and told Jake's teacher what was going on. In a few minutes, Jake came out of the bathroom fully clothed and went back to his class. Since this happened right at the end of the day, Jake just made it onto the bus for his ride home.

Right after school, I went down to the principal's office and related the incident to her. She told me I shouldn't have let him go home. That since he was behaving so strangely, he might have been high on something. I agreed, but having had some experience with this boy and being in a bit of a state of shock myself, I knew he was quite strange already and didn't think he was a danger to himself or others. I just wanted to get him home. If I had to do it all over again, even though it was the end of the school day, I would have walked him down to the office and let the administration handle it right then and there. As it turned out, Jake came to school the next day, met with the admin and some guidance counselors, and that's the last I heard of the event.

Public school is life. It is messy and unpredictable. Some kids come to school with all kinds of hang-ups and depressions. For some, the last thing on their minds is learning math or reading. We definitely need more counselors in the schools. As it is, we often split a counselor between two schools and think that'll work just fine. It doesn't. I understand the money crunch on public schools and I don't have a funding answer. What I do have is experience and the perspective that we don't do enough to counsel our troubled students. As difficult as it is, if we don't get these kids help when they're young, society's burden will only increase as they get older.

Society's burden . . an interesting phrase, isn't it? I sound like Scrooge talking about the "surplus population." How would you like to be labeled "society's burden?" These disturbed kids are your kids and my kids. They're our children. They are not a burden. They are kids with problems they can't fix on their own. They are precious and very difficult. They need our help, not our pity. While they're young, they're still growing emotionally and physically. There is no better time to help them overcome psychological issues than when they are still becoming. My heart goes out to kids like Jake. They're kids who come from homes that are so dysfunctional and unstable they have two strikes against them before they even get into the batter's box. But even with two strikes, they're not out yet. Though the challenges are enormous, we can do better. We can do better than one counselor for 500 kids on a biweekly visiting schedule.

Are we really doing all we can to help those in need? Or are we hiding behind tax cuts and the ignorant notion, "Why don't they just pull themselves up by the bootstraps and get a job!" I've seen mental illness up close. It's like asking someone to pull up their bootstraps when they aren't wearing any boots.

A few months ago, I was at a stoplight and saw a disheveled young man looking through a garbage can near a strip mall market. He was wearing oversized grey sweatpants that he had to hold with one hand just to keep them up. Then I saw his sweats drop to the ground and he looked like he was wearing some sort of adult diaper. I turned the corner and I stopped. I couldn't get the picture of that man fumbling around with his sweatpants out of my mind. He just looked so helpless and confused. I stopped the car, turned around, and got out to help him. As I approached, he looked a little off, scruffy faced and jittery, still holding onto his sweatpants. I said something like, "Hey Man, are you okay? Can I help you with something?"

He looked up at me and said, "I went in the store, but I need two quarters."

I opened my wallet and all I had was two bucks. "What's your name?" I asked.

"Michael Caine," he said and I thought of the famous actor.

"Well, Michael, all I have here is two bucks, but I hope that's enough."

He took the money and went into the store. I got back into my car and as I drove around, I cried. Who is there to care for a poor soul like Michael? What was he like in high school? Middle school? What would his past teachers think of Michael's fate today? In the end, he reminded me of Jake. Somehow, I know we can do better. We can't save the world, but we can make it a better place than it is right now.

Over the years—and since that day with Jake—I've been asked many times by other teachers and administrators to check out the boys' bathroom. Believe me, whenever I heard that question, I knew I could be in for a lot more than I planned. Now that I'm retired, like the Pinball Wizard, I've passed my pinball crown on to the next generation of unsuspecting teachers caught near the bathroom at the wrong time. Hey, newly hired teacher, there's some kind of commotion going on in the bathroom. Mind checking it out?

BROKEN ARROW

The Vietnam War movie *We Were Soldiers* has a powerful scene wherein Lt. Col. Hal Moore's platoon is overrun by the Viet Cong. The enemy is infiltrating his camp from all directions and defeat is imminent. All hell was breaking loose. There is a great scene where the camera pans 360 degrees from Moore's perspective and we see the utter futility of the battle. The enemy has penetrated their defenses from every direction and they are being overrun. The colonel then grittily utters this infamous command to his radio operator:

"Broken Arrow!"

Lt. Col. Moore, played by Mel Gibson, has used the one command that will immediately divert all available resources to come to his aid. This order is never to be used lightly, and only under the most dire of circumstances is it to be considered.

So why are we talking about famous military terms in a sixth grade teacher's memoirs? Because, my dear friend, we in the public schools, are also at war. Not a war between teachers and students. Not a war between parents and teachers. Not even a war between the staff and the administration. No sir, we are at war with unwanted conversations!

You've heard them, you even try to avoid them, but you all too often fail and are left tethered to your desk or cemented in the hallway, utterly locked into a conversation you do not want to be having. You feel the sweat on your brow as the clock ticks and you think of all the things you need to prepare for while this staff member has grossly overestimated the extent of your interest in the subject he or she is more than willing to expound upon. You think, "Why does Sally think I have *any* interest in this? I have ten minutes left to get papers run off and my room arranged for my sixth hour experiment and I'm standing in the hallway talking with Sally! Doesn't she see by my expression this conversation has absolutely no relevance to my life? How can I be smiling when all I want to do is strangle her? Do I look like some human electrical outlet that's begging for Sally to plug her venting fan into?"

As the pressure mounts and precious seconds are sucked into that vortex of a mouth that never stops moving, our survival instincts kick in and we look for an escape. It's strange how a conversation that is this boring can cause such anxiety because of a time crunch. Our heightened senses and peripheral vision scan the hallways in hopes of transferring the unwanted conversation to any negligent, unsuspecting fellow teacher. At this point in our precarious imprisonment, we will do anything to break free from this psychological torture. There is nothing too low to stoop to, no promise we will not make or break, no friend or family member who wouldn't look great under a bus.

If we are fortunate enough, the bell will ring, or a passerby will be caught in the verbal fly paper and we will be free to sprint to our classroom or at least free to contemplate that being on the Titanic wouldn't have been such a bad thing.

PTSD has nothing on PTUCS (Post Traumatic Unwanted Conversation Syndrome). For those suffering from PTUCS, (isn't it really all of us?) the symptoms are premature greying of the hair, erupting facial tics, and the ability to execute a 180 degree turn midstride in the hallway upon spotting a potential lock down conversational candidate.

At our middle school, in between our in-service meetings, our department meetings, our house meetings, our grade level meetings, and our IEP meetings, we initiated a clandestine grass roots movement to combat this form of psychological abuse. Grafting in military terminology seemed like the right thing to do, so POW and Broken Arrow in the school setting were born.

If a teacher has been in a lock down conversation with another staff member, you could say you were "POW'd," a prisoner of war. We soon adapted the term to include the name of the initiating offender. Thus, if Paul had locked you into a conversation, you could say you were a POP'd, or a Prisoner of Paul. Since many names don't make the acronym sound snappy, POW'd was the default usage.

Now this collegial verbal venting or after-the-fact acknowledgment of the attack did provide some relief from serious and long-term psychological damage, but it was viewed more as a Band Aid, not a cure. As the movement continued to develop its charter of psychological warfare terms, "Broken Arrow" came into vogue.

In the school setting, if a teacher was at his or her desk in a lock down conversation, if possible, a quick email with the subject line "Broken Arrow" could be sent. This emergency email could be acted upon with a quick visit from another teacher in the doorway of the classroom saying, "Hey Bill, we've got a meeting right now in E-11." Or an office aide could pipe into the classroom loudspeaker and say, "Mrs. Burns, you've got a parent call on line six." Any way to break the invisible grip on our conversations was deemed healthy and wanted. If conversationally ensnared in the hallway, a finger could be wiggled to a teacher passing by, signaling a broken finger and thus, a Broken Arrow situation. The teacher passing by could then remind you of a curriculum meeting or that he or she needed you for a minute to discuss something very important.

Occasionally, I have been involved in conversations with fellow staff members about PTUCS. Advice has been freely offered to confront, in a kindly, "I want to help you out" manner, those who habitually initiate extended unwanted conversations. The purist of motives being to help them gain self-awareness that this situation is taking place and is counterproductive to developing friendships in the workplace. While this advice sounds valid, worthwhile, and probably has numerous research studies to back it up, I only seem to offer it to others and not take advantage of it myself. Having taught the properties of density for many years to my sixth graders, I've often recounted the fact that social awareness density levels have been left unattended in our physical science textbooks. I am reminded of a Gary Larson cartoon, in which a professor with pointing stick in hand is illustrating the technique of inserting a giant flat head screwdriver into the single groove of a screwhead to a class of befuddled Cro-Magnons. I guess I thought if I ever confronted a lock-down entity and tried to explain the unintentional torture they were inflicting on all human life, I'd only make them angry and prompt them to better explain their feelings on the subject at our next meeting. Better to play dumb and look for an easy exit.

As we now leave the conversational battlefield, let us rally around the banner of kindness, patience, and objectivity. If we see a colleague in need, let us offer our assistance, and cry "Broken Arrow!" Or turn tail, run, and abandon the hostage. My final piece of advice, gleaned from years of unwanted conversations, is this, my flummoxed friend: the next time we're talking to someone in the hallways or at our desk and they seem to be a little preoccupied or distant and are wiggling their fingers to all passersby, let our own awareness be kindled that perhaps, we are the perpetrator, not the prisoner of war!

THE LAST RACE

As a kid, I loved to race and sprint whenever I could. Growing up with four older brothers on the northwest side of Milwaukee, Wisconsin in the 1960s, we were always in some sport season, year-round: baseball in the summer, football in the fall and winter, and basketball in the winter and spring. Our backyard was big enough for a football field. The open field next to our house was perfect for a baseball diamond and a rough, dirt-court basketball hoop was set up near the clothes line where my mom would hang up our washed clothes to dry.

Many epic sports battles took place on these hallowed fields of my youth. There was the time my brother broke my collarbone when we were playing tag football and he shoved me out of bounds into the trunk of an apricot tree. Or the time during a friendly neighborhood tackle football game, when Crazy Peter got angry and stomped his heavy work boots within an inch of my brother's head. Understanding that I ate and slept sports as a kid, that I loved competition, that I set sprint and hurdling records as a high schooler and collegiate athlete, will help you keenly feel the depth of my humiliation in the story I am about to relate. It may cut off a few minutes of my personal teacher's hell video, so here we go . .

It was a beautiful spring day in Wisconsin, which means it was probably about forty-seven degrees and sunny with a biting wind coming off of Lake Michigan. We were nearing the end of another middle school track season. Being the hurdle coach, I was standing close to the starting line of the track, running my hurdlers through some starting drills near the end of a Friday practice. Another coach had just blown his whistle indicating practice was over and it was time to head off the track and back to school to pack up and catch the buses home. As two of my hurdlers were coming back to the starting line, one of them said, "Hey Coach, let's race before we go home!"

Well, there you have it. Marty McFly was just called a chicken. Apollo Creed just told Rocky to stay down on the mat. Agent Smith cranked his neck while Neo beckoned him with fingers. How could I say no?

That's just it! I've said no a hundred times. I'm a track coach. I've taught kids every day of my coaching career that you don't race unless you're totally warmed up. How many times did I see kids wearing a T-shirt and shorts in forty degree weather, dinking around in the bleachers ten minutes before a race? "Get out there and start warming up!" I'd yell. "If you don't feel a sweat on your brow before the race, then you are not ready to compete! You'll pull a muscle for sure if you're not properly warmed up!" These are things I've said a million times.

So why didn't I take my own advice that chilly day so long ago? Who knows? I was cold, stiff, and forty-eight years old. I was not warmed up. I hadn't done any kind of hurdle or sprint race in years. All I needed to say was, "Sorry kids. I'm not warmed up and you've got to get going or you'll miss your bus." Or "I only compete against Olympic caliber athletes." So what did this veteran sprint and hurdle coach of twenty-five years, knowing full well of the consequences of such an irrational impulsive challenge, say to those bright smiling faces?

"Let's do this."

The three of us took our lanes at the starting line of the 110-meter low hurdles. The white-haired guy took the middle lane and was flanked by eight graders' Kenny on the left and Troy on the right. Before this race begins, let me add here that one of these boys went on to set his high school record in the 110-meter high hurdles and was a Wisconsin state track and field finalist two years in a row, and the other boy was a state finalist in the 200-meter dash. These two were not your average eight grade tracksters.

I suppose as I relaxed my shoulders and bent my head down to concentrate on the start of the race, these thoughts may have crossed my mind: "What are you doing? Are you nuts? Do you revel in humiliation? How can this turn out well? If you win, they'll be mad. If you lose, they'll gloat." And then there was that tiny coach in my head whispering in the background, "You're not warmed up. You know what happens when you race without warming up . . "

I discarded all those voices of reason and at the bleat of another coaches' whistle, the race was on. Being the focused competitor that I am, I never looked right or left as we approached the first hurdle, but as we cleared it, I felt just behind both runners. As my lead foot planted and my trail leg snapped around and down onto the track, I had the immediate racer's impulse to accelerate, shift into the highest gear, and make up that half meter I had fallen behind.

As I mentally shifted into overdrive, I physically felt a pull in my left hamstring. Now the race shifted into a *Twilight-Zone* dream sequence. Hurdling is a unique race in that it is made up of barriers that you race between. Whether or not you choose to navigate the barriers, the barriers exist and will assert their presence, whether you try to go over them or not. I would often tell the kids that if their lead or trail leg was too low, the hurdle would remind them of this fact in no uncertain terms. I was in for a big reminder.

As I approached the second hurdle, I felt no strength in my left leg as I tried to push off and over the hurdle. The next few moments were a blur as my lead leg somehow tangled into the hurdle and I went sprawling head first onto the track. I must've rolled a few times and ended up, seated on the track, bruised, scraped, and humiliated. Kenny and Troy came back and tried to help me up, but I had torn my left hamstring and sprained my throbbing right ankle, so neither leg would support my weight. Another assistant coach rolled over the shot put cart, helped me in, and carted me off the track to my car. One of the clearest memories I have of this ordeal is of the head girl's coach laughing at the sight of me being wheeled off the track, unable to stand up on my own. Thanks, Coach!

Oh, the story doesn't end there. The hospital x-rayed my ankle and said nothing was broken and that my hamstring would heal without surgery. For the next five weeks I hobbled around, my limping a constant invitation for others to ask me how I had injured myself and the prideful, humiliating racer's tale would begin again and again. During those five weeks, the pain in my ankle would not subside. I had sprained my ankles many times before and knew the healing process, but this pain would not go away. This seemed odd.

Finally, I went to a podiatrist, retold the tale of woe, and had him x-ray my ankle again. Sure enough, he said, "Yeah, you've got two broken chips. One on each side of the ankle, but since it's already been five weeks, we'll just put you in an aircast and give it another week or two to finish healing."

What is to be learned from this sordid tale of misery and pride? Listen to your own advice, Coach. Take your own medicine. Pride comes before the fall . . literally. Warm yourself up before you race, Old Man. Or perhaps, Captain Kirk said it best to Dr. McCoy, "Galavanting around the cosmos is a game for the young, Doctor!" Or racing around a frigid track during a Wisconsin spring, Coach Shurilla!

THE FLYING TANK

When I was around forty-three years old, I was inspired to research into my father's World War II experiences as a bombardier aboard a B-17 in the United States' 8th Air Force. My father died of a heart attack when I was fifteen years old and I never had a lot of discussions with him about his war stories before he passed. All I really knew was that he had flown fifteen bombing missions over Germany, was shot down and spent fifteen months as a POW in a Nazi prison camp.

Also, around this time, I was part of a new committee to develop a Veteran's Day Program at our middle school. As I researched my father's 306th Bomber Group, interviewed his former bunkmate in the Nazi prison camp, and read captain's reports of the damage his plane underwent during those combat missions, I began to gain a deep respect for the price he and others paid to liberate the world from the grip of Nazi tyranny. Also, as I was researching, I made many contacts with other baby boomers, who, like me, were delving into their parents' past and trying to understand a period in their lives like no other—a world at war.

While I was going through my father's squadron journals and other artifacts, I met a woman by the name of Nancy Thayer-Haggerty. Nancy had been doing similar research on her father and she asked me, "Larry, haven't you ever talked to Bob Tank? He lives right in Menomonee Falls with you and he was in the same prison camp as your dad: Stalag Luft I!"

"I've never met him," I replied, "but I'd love to talk with him!" Nancy gave me Bob Tank's information. I called him up, arranged a meeting, and went over to his house, about a four-minute drive from my own!

Bob Tank was quite a character. With an unbelievably gravelly voice and an infectious laugh, Bob shared with me many memories of the war and of the experiences he had with my dad. It seems they both went to the same bombardier school in Texas, were both shot down on bombing missions, and both ended up as POWs in Stalag Luft I, or as Bob liked to call it, "Barth on the Baltic!" Barth, Germany, near the Baltic Sea coast, was the closest city to the prison camp. Bob also related to me that he was the Air Force's only "Flying Tank."

Bob made particular mention of the discussion he had with my dad at the camp, wherein they both pledged to take in a University of Wisconsin versus Marquette University sporting event when they returned to the states. Bob was a big UW supporter and my dad was a big Marquette fan. Unfortunately, those two never got together after the war, even though they spent many years living only a few miles from one another. Apparently, The Greatest Generation had other things to do besides hooking up with old prison camp buddies.

Now back to the formation of the Veterans' program at my school. With all the recently acquired information about World War II fresh in my mind, I was anxious to see our middle school participate in a program honoring the veterans in our community. Our principal formed a committee and a planning meeting was held. We decided to pattern our program after a neighboring community's existing one. Our highest priority was to instill in our student body an understanding of the cost of freedom and the highest amount of respect for all our veterans. We included in our program the presentation of the American flag by a color guard made up of local veterans, our school's eight grade chorus, the school band, a military veteran keynote speaker, laying of the wreaths, a short video clip from *Saving Private Ryan*, and a community video made up of veterans' pictures brought in by their children and grandchildren with inspiring music playing in the background.

The veterans' program was a huge success and has been repeated at my school every year for the past sixteen years. With an understanding of the background of this program, it's time to share another one of my special memories.

With the passing of my father at such a young age (fifty-seven), I was never truly able to thank him for so many things. Not the least of which would be his service to our country. So after a few years of our veterans' program at the middle school, I hatched a plan to not only honor my father for his extraordinary military service and sacrifice, but to also honor the Air Force's only recorded Flying Tank!

At our request, Bob Tank, along with many other community veterans, had been attending our veterans' program for a number of years. Bob had also spoken to my classroom about the war and at many other venues during this time. Being on the planning committee, it was easy for me to volunteer as the keynote speaker and present a tribute to Bob.

On the day of the program, the gymnasium was filled to the brim with all three grade levels (sixth through eighth), school board members, district dignitaries, the band, the chorus, military veterans, administrators, etc. all present. The attendance was well over a thousand people in a small gym with one set of bleachers.

Before I spoke, we played a video excerpt from the movie *Memphis Belle*, which showcased a World War II B-17 crew and their perils over Germany during their final mission. With the image of the B-17 fresh in the minds of the audience, I began my speech and chronicled the military life of Bob Tank and the harrowing story of his plane's demise, his capture, interrogation, and subsequent imprisonment at Stalag Luft I.

With a story this compelling, even middle schoolers gave their utmost attention. It's not every day you're in the presence of someone who actually parachuted out of a burning plane at 20,000 feet, who heard the German Shepherd guard dogs barking while patrolling the prison camp, who watched the light knife through the wooden window slats from the bright, panning search lights as he lay on his sawdust mattress at night.

As I told Bob Tanks' story, I was really telling the story of my father as well. Their stories were so similar. Everything I related about Bob's wartime experience was akin to my own father's. As I neared the end of my speech, I had planned for Bob to stand and receive the applause he so much deserved, but the audience beat me to the punch. In the last few lines of my speech I said, "And now I present to you, a World War II veteran, a man who survived two years in a Nazi prison camp, Robert H. Tank . . "

Before I could finish my speech, the audience stood and thunderously applauded. The eighty-something Bob Tank, with arthritic knees aching, slowly and humbly stood, took off his hat, and waved to the crowd. I will never forget that moment. There was a bright spotlight, not a searchlight, on Bob. So many people were clapping, whistling, and cheering. He so deserved that tribute and I thought of my dad and felt that moment was his as well. It was the best I could do for him. I looked down at my speech and knew I would never be able to finish it, to say the last two words publicly, so I whispered them to myself. The last line of my speech was, "And now I present to you, a World War II veteran, a man who survived two years in a Nazi prison camp, Robert H. Tank . . my friend."

THE COLOR OF BREATH

A number of times during my teaching career, I would say to myself and hear other teachers remark as well, "I have got to keep a journal of all the crazy things kids say! Do you know what Megan said today? . . "

Well, I didn't keep that journal, and as I now look back, I can only remember a handful of those uniquely phrased utterings of the middle school mind. But believe me, they happen on a fairly regular basis. Maybe it's because of the frequency and how busy we are that we just laugh, shake our heads, and move on with the day muttering, "I have got to keep a journal!" Yet we never do. We don't take the time to write them down.

Of course, there are the typical verbal mistakes in science class; words that few sixth grade classmates pick up on, but give the teachers a smirk.

For example, a student giving an oral report on an ocean biome or reading some expository text may say, "And the octopus' eight testicles (tentacles) grabbed the unsuspecting prey." Or the much more commonly rendered, "Now the female orgasm (organism), unlike the male of this species, exhibits many unusual characteristics."

Not all the memorable quotes are funny. I remember jogging around the track one day at a track practice with a runner straggling behind the pack. I said something like, "How's it going, Rita? You look kinda down."

To which she replied, "My parents are getting divorced."

Thud. How do you respond to that? This girl's life was in for a major upheaval. She knew it. I knew it. But neither one of us really knew what it would be like, just that it was going to hurt an awful lot. Sometimes just jogging around the track with someone who cares can help.

Can you imagine remembering a quote uttered from a twelve-year-old boy, a good twenty years after the fact? Must be a pretty impressive quote. Inspirational, deep, thought-provoking, words laced with adolescent wisdom. A dear friend of mine once said, "You can't stay young forever, Larry, but you can be immature for a lifetime!" With that in mind, here's one of my favorite sixth grade quotes. Simple. Absurd. To the point. Ultimately, middle school.

I remember standing near the door of my room, near where the folding wall that separated my room from the next had its locking handle. The passing bell had just rung and some students were leaving the room while some were entering for the next hour. Two boys were standing near the folding door, when one of them said to the other, with a sour look on his face, "Yer breath stink, Ricky." Note the lack of an exclamation mark.

It was said with candor and it elicited no response from Ricky, other than a look of disgust and, "Shut Up, Zach!"

To this day, it is one of the funniest lines I remember. I have often used it out of nowhere, in a casual text to my teacher friend who also knew both students, just because. He has heard me use it for many a year and, of course, it needs no explanation. It is just purely middle school. Cruel. Spontaneous. All filters removed. Funny.

So, for all those teachers thinking, "I've got to write this stuff down before I forget" I say, go right ahead and write it down. Keep a journal of all those crazy things kids say. The funny, the absurd, the profound . . write them all down! These are moments in time that soon wash away along with the faces and places where they occurred. You'll be glad you did.

And let me add an ominous warning: if you don't record the more eloquent expressions uttered by your less articulate adolescent apprentices, you may find yourself at some future date standing nose to nose in a congested elevator with an onion-chewing, cigarette-smoking, coffee-guzzling businessman, and the only thought that will come to mind will be, "Yer breath stink, Ricky."

Since we're on the topic of bad breath, let me share a quick thought on the subject. I used to joke with a friend and ask, "What if breath had color, like a visible color to breath vapor? What color is my breath?" Some answers could be lime green, yellow with purple flecks, black. It was quite difficult to come up with a favorable color to assign breath, even mine.

On a more positive note, if breath did have color, one could be walking down the hallways at school and notice a gaggle of teachers gathered with vapor clouds of green, orange, and black spewing from their mouths like volcanic vents on the deep ocean floor. A clear sign to steer hard to starboard and avoid this cackling crowd at all costs.

In summary, kids say the darnedest things. Keeping a journal of these spontaneous verbal combustions will bring a glow to your heart in years to come. In the future, whether standing in an elevator, walking down the hallways, or trying to turn away from someone's malodorously brown breath, having more than "Yer breath stink, Ricky," as a go-to thought may provide a mental shield as effective as an antiseptic wipe. On the other hand, maybe that's all you'll ever really need!

Oh, and if by chance you're wondering, Zach was right; Ricky's breath did stink. Probably a forest green tinted with a dash of ebony.

AND THE OSCAR GOES TO . .

As a teacher, have you ever given a poor lesson and felt like you had just permanently corrupted the art of teaching and despite all warning labels, induced educational vomiting in your students? I know I have, and by the look of it, so have most, if not all teachers at one point or another in their teaching careers.

I can distinctly recall butchering a math lesson, immediately heading to the hallways for a between classes therapy session with my colleagues, and then uttering, "That was the worst gosh awful lesson in the history of public education! If the principal had walked in on my last period, I would be strung up on the nearest tree for gross educational neglect! If awards were given out for the crappiest lesson of the year, I just won an Oscar!"

Okay, okay, enough already! Here's the point. We all make mistakes. No student is perfect. No teacher is perfect. We strive to teach as many quality lessons as possible in our 180 days—or roughly 900 lessons—a school year. Imagine performing to the same crowd for 180 days in a row. Now that would be a tough crowd! And yet that is precisely what a school teacher does year in and year out. That's why you keep careful lesson plans, throw out the lessons that don't work, and keep tweaking the ones that do.

Since we teach our kids every year there are "no self put-downs" allowed in the classroom, we decided that should carry over into our own teacher conversation vernacular. After commiserating in the hallways and sharing our teaching flubs over and over again, we all reached the point where we would say to each other, "Okay, no more self put-downs!" Of course, we would say this *after* we had vented, but just the act of saying that simple phrase was cathartic and checked our negativity in its tracks.

Not only should we check the negativity, we should replace it with positive affirmations. However insincere we may be, the iteration of constructive self-talk points our attitudes in the right direction and lessens the debilitating effects of a crappy lesson. For example, after rotting the minds of your kids for fifty minutes and self-verbalizing the disdain for your own teaching, you might say, "Okay, that lesson really sucked, but I've got four more chances to make it right today!" Or "I hope future science never has access to the lesson I just taught, but I did get Jimmy to laugh for the first time in weeks . . even if it was *at* my lesson!"

Whenever I'm in a situation where I have to do something I really have no interest in doing, I recall what a wise friend once told me.

"Larry, all you have to do is act like you really *like* to do what you *have* to do and in time, you will find it's not so bad." In other words, "Fake it till you make it!" That works in teaching too. When you are really feeling down and low energy, you taught a foul lesson, or you're just not in the mood to teach, remember you are a professional and do your job. Act like the lesson is the greatest morsel of wisdom you've ever fed your students and you'll soon find that it may not be food for the gods, but it's not half bad. They may even learn something today.

The next time you meet up with one of your favorite colleagues in the hallway between classes and he looks like he was just run over by a freight train, expect him to say, "After that last lesson, I am living proof that the mind and the mouth can have absolutely no connection whatsoever!" But also be ready to pull out your social skills trump card and say, "Hey Mr. S., no self put-downs!" Well, at least remember to say that after you've finished venting yourself.

TAKE A KNEE

If you happen to be involved in coaching for any length of time, you will invariably meet up with a couple of coaching characters. Of course, some of them will stick out for the wrong reasons, like they get caught drinking beer out of their car trunks at an away meet or they're obnoxiously over-confident as their team kicks your butt year after year. Hopefully, however, at least once or twice, you'll come across the stuff of legends: a Vince Lombardi, John Wooden or as Chris Farley would muse dreamy-eyed while chewing on a fresh piece of summer sausage, "Ditka!"

Enter Coach C.

Stocky, average height, handle bar moustache, eyebrows your fingers would get snarled in if your hand got too close, thinning pate, and his most distinguishing feature of all, the voice. How to describe his voice? If you were setting a Moog synthesizer to replicate the sound, the settings would be something like "rock tumbler," "bass boost," and "mega volume." His whispers could probably carry 100 yards into the wind. Forever clad in an oversized, unbuttoned wind breaker, stopwatch and whistle dangling from his neck, with clipboard in hand, Coach C. would nervously pace up and down the inner, grassy part of a track and holler encouragement to his athletes.

In order to grasp the "true grit" of this middle school track and field icon (even without an eyepatch), permit me to relate an early season track invitational experience. Every spring on a Saturday morning, Coach C.'s middle school would host a track and field invitational and invite all the area middle schools to the feast. I call it a feast because that is what the meat .. I mean "meet" was to his team. Each year Coach C.'s team (which we'll call Park Middle School) would dominate the scoring from start to finish. Over and over again, Park Middle School's name would be blasted over the loudspeakers. "First place in the long jump .. Park Middle School. First place in the hurdles .. Park Middle School. First place in the 400-meter relay .. Park Middle School." If you're anything like me, after reading that last line you probably already hate Park Middle School. They were to middle school track what the New England Patriots have been to pro football. Too bad there weren't any footballs to deflate; we couldn't find a good excuse for losing to them so much!

So here I am with my fellow track coaches up in the press box at the event scratch meeting, jamming Dunkin Donuts into my mouth just before the meet is set to begin, when I hear that booming voice down on the infield below. As I glance out the open window, white powdered sugar cascading off my lips and down my shirt, I see Coach C. with his entire team gathered around him, like Jesus giving the Sermon on the Mount.

Coach C. was taking attendance.

"Ace Johnson?"

"Here."

"Gene Wilkins?"

"Here"

"Peter Jenkins?"

Silence.

"Peter Jenkins?!"

More silence, and then a quivering voice from the back of the pack, "Uhh, Jenkins said he couldn't make it."

Coach C. lifted his left eyebrow, took his eyes off the clipboard, and stared out into the crowd with a look of a shark spying a dangling leg off a surfboard.

"Jenkins told me he would be here today." Then a few more moments of awkward silence. "If you can't take a man at his word, you can't take him for much."

And there it was, a glimpse into the soul of Coach C. Old School, hard knocks, brass knuckle truth. A coach's quip uttered without preparation. It was habit. Real world truths rolled off Coach C.'s tongue like chocolate candies off Lucille Ball's confectionary conveyer belt.

When Coach C. completed taking attendance, he barked, "Take a knee." All the athletes, male and female, knelt down on the infield grass and Coach C. proceeded to give a short heartfelt prayer invoking protection on all the athletes and giving thanks for the beauty of the day and the blessing of healthy bodies with which to compete. I loved it. You just don't see that kind of thing much anymore.

Whenever we competed against Coach C.'s team, I would always look forward to any interaction with him, hoping to hear one of those crusty crabs scamper out of his mouth. I've always thought we need more coaches like Coach C. Men and women who teach responsibility, dedication, and honor by word and example. Our youth desperately need icons of stability and virtue by which to pattern their lives or at least, get started on the right foot. Too many coaches today coach for a year or two and then drop out. Coach C. coached for over thirty years! Thank God for all the coaches like Coach C. out there—those compassionate souls who love kids and would do anything to help them prepare for the rigors of life, sacrificing a major portion of their own lives doing it.

Before we leave the Park Middle School track, let me share one last quote. This was uttered by one of Coach C.'s assistant coaches. This guy always wore a baseball cap pulled tightly down onto his head, dark sunglasses, and a bushy moustache. He would stand with his arms folded in the third turn of the track, waiting for his 400-meter runner to enter the home stretch and then yell, "Turn the screw!"

Where do these guys come up with this stuff? "Turn the Screw?!" Are we in metal shop class? Maybe he meant, "Tame the Shrew?!" Wait a minute, that's Shakespeare. No way that dude was quoting Shakespeare. I guess the shop quote is more likely. We took it to mean "kick it in gear" or "turn it on" or "increasing speed at this point in the race will surely apply pressure to the other runners and will likely assure victory." Yeah, I know. He wasn't thinking that last one.

You can imagine my fellow coaches and I would use that phrase with abandon and in many contexts. We might be sitting in some ungodly boring faculty meeting, lean over to one another, and whisper, "Turn the screw," or come upon a fellow teacher reaming out a naughty student in the hallways. "Turn the screw, baby, turn the screw!"

By the way, I'm still afraid of what might have happened when old Peter Jenkins showed up at the next Park Middle School track practice, nonchalantly bopping in with his earbuds firmly plugged in, listening to Kiss. "You know, Peter, if you can't take a man at his word . . "

I think it's time to take a knee, Mr. Jenkins.

TODAY IS A FREE DAY

In my never-ending attempt to make the lives of my teacher friends more enjoyable—or in other words, another joke that I liked to pull—I introduced the invocation of a free day for their classroom. Now you may be wondering what the blazes is a "free day" and how on earth was I endowed with the power to grant this blessing upon my co-workers? These, my friend, are very good questions and while the answers may seem simple enough, they are rife with complexity.

Imagine if you will, walking into any middle school classroom and seeing the typical "Daily Objectives" listed on the whiteboard. Goals like, "The student will create a bar graph from data gleaned in the membrane lab" Or "The student will demonstrate mastery of the four sentence types in an expository paragraph." Now these are the white stuffing of middle school Oreo boredom, the type of white board objectives that become white noise in our middle schoolers' mind, the type of speech uttered by Charlie Brown's teacher in a muted trumpet. In other words, teachers really write these objectives on the board so their observing principal can note them on their iPads' lesson reviewing software during an unscheduled classroom drop-in, not because our eager students are craving pre-lesson nourishment in an anticipatory set.

Herein lies the power of the free day! Since the daily written objectives become so mundane and overlooked, one can easily and secretly insert, "Today is a free day!" on a fellow teacher's whiteboard, where once loomed a concrete learning objective. Once planted, the free day objective festers like a giant zit on the greasy face of the white board until one of our overzealous students notices it and gives it a quick squeeze.

Once the hidden gem is discovered, the student must quickly extrapolate the meaning of such an objective. Today is a free day! What could this possibly mean? Does it mean I can run around the room and push classmates' books on the floor? Does it mean there is going to be a party with candy, ice cream, cake, and balloons? Could it possibly mean no homework, board games, computer time, and hair pulling contests? Make no mistake, once a middle schooler grabs hold of the "free day" concept, anything is a possibility.

Now that the student has begun to concoct the meaning of this "free day," the inevitable will happen, and this is by far, my favorite part. The student's mind, filled with grandiose delusions of the free day, must corroborate the truthfulness of this impossibly delicious dessert. He must shake off the blissful cloak of unbridled happiness this free day has clothed him in and he must, inevitably, ask the teacher if this is true. Is today really a free day?

Now the teacher, sitting at his or her desk or standing in the doorway waiting for class to begin, is completely unaware of the classroom management mayhem the free day objective has created. He stands oblivious, enjoying the two and half minutes of non-supervision that passing time affords him, until a student's excited face is thrust into his own while joyfully asking, "Mr. Schmidt, is today a free day?!"

At this precise moment, a lifetime of evil thoughts pass through our teacher's mind. He may think to himself, in the time-warping microsecond that brain firing neurons provide:

"Shurilla wrote, 'Today is a free day!' on my board again. This excited child is soon going to be let down, severely. I hope no one else saw the 'free day' sign or the whole class will be in an uproar. I'm going to kill him."

After the initial wave of hostility passes over the furrowed brow of our befuddled teacher, he must kindly smile at the eagerly anticipating student and say something like, "Well, Jimmy, today really isn't a free day. Mr. Shurilla just likes to play a joke on me now and then and this is one of those times." Jimmy, utterly dejected, hands at his side, must return to his molded plastic chair, slowly shuffling his once energized feet, and slink back into his seat, defeated.

To the casual observer, this joke may seem like cruel and unusual punishment on a middle school level, but let me reassure you, nothing could be farther from the truth. The student was actually given a moment of unbridled happiness in an otherwise dismal day. While today may not have been a free day, when *will* it occur? What will happen on that happy day? Is tomorrow a free day? What does Mary think the free day will be like? Has anyone else had a free day this year? Yes, the free day objective spurs the creativity of our pre-adolescents' minds and gives them one more good reason to come to school. Yeah, learning is okay, but today might be a free day. At least, that's what Mr. Schmidt's white board says. Pass it on. By the way, you better get back to your own classroom and check your whiteboard, quick! You left your door unlocked when you went to the office ..

SURVIVAL

Invariably, when one is writing a memoir about a middle school teaching career, the subject of vomiting will come up. Okay, it's not invariable and may *never* come up when middle school education is discussed, but if you ever did throw up in school, you will remember it for a lifetime. And if you had a classmate puke his or her guts out, you may be emotionally scarred from the close proximity to the bile blast.

Sure, I've had a handful of kids come up to my desk over the years and say, "Mr. Shurilla, I don't feel so goo .. " and then haul off to the waste basket to make a quick deposit, but there's nothing special in that. It happens all the time. However, as I look back, there is one hurl episode that comes to mind not only for its ferocity, but also for its humanity.

It began as a school day like any other that year. Teach math, teach math again, teach science, eat lunch, teach science again, have a prep period, and then end the day with reading. This particular group of students was reading from a survival series that contained stories of mountain storms, inner city racial conflicts, and airplane crash landings. We could've added our own survival chapter titled: Upchuck, Stomach Macaroni, or for the high-brow readers, The Nemesis of Emesis.

Somewhere in the middle of the period, a skinny white kid with limited academic ability, but one who excelled in humility and guilelessness— in other words the type of kid the "cool kids" loved to pick on—happened to be sitting in the front row directly in front of me as I was teaching. Being the consummately observant professional educator that I was, I noticed that "Carl" was looking rather ashen. Instead of asking him how he felt, I did what any award-winning classroom teacher would do, I ignored my instincts and called on him to read aloud. This Carl did with instant obedience, but something was off. He began to stop reading intermittently and had a surprised look on his face, as if he was discovering a primordial urge, a repulsive yet basic human survival instinct. By the time I realized what was happening, it was far too late. Carl's throat began a kind of rhythmic worm dance, not unlike the dinner scene from the first Alien movie, and then the first eruption began. Picture a vomit bazooka firing a deadly spread in a 180-degree arc around the front of the room. Simultaneously, every other student recoiled amid groans of horror, and shoved their chairs away from ground zero, leaving Carl alone, soaking in his vomit bath.

There was a momentary pause, allowing Carl to reload, and the second saliva salvo commenced. Ever a scientist, I recall being startled that so much vomit could come out of one individual. When the fallout settled and all bile batteries were emptied, I immediately came to Carl's rescue by running to the call button on the wall, calling the office, and asking that a custodian be dispensed to Room N-9, ASAP!

Now for the humanity.

This particular group of students was known for picking on each other. I expected a lot of complaining and comments like, "You are so gross, Carl! Sick, Carl! Get out of here, man! That smells sooooo foul!" Much to my pleasure and surprise, a black kid I'll call Zach, known to be one of the biggest teasers in the group, gently approached Carl from behind, put his hand on the one dry spot of Carl's shoulder and said, "It's all right, man. It'll be all right." The room was silent. It felt like a real life Willy Wonka was holding the everlasting gobstopper and saying, "So shines a good deed in a weary world." And thus, it was.

The class remained quiet. The custodian came, spread, and swept up his magical tan powder as Carl was escorted by another student down to the nurse's room. I never heard any of the kids make fun of Carl for that episode. Sometimes, even amid a crisis situation, the kids will rise above it all and teach us grown-ups about kindness and humanity. Thanks, Zach. It doesn't have to take a foreign battlefield or Super Bowl comeback to elicit our moral courage. Sometimes, all you need is a classroom of diverse kids, reading about survival and seeing a friend in need. Yeah, Carl, it really will be all right.

CUSTODIANS OF EDUCATION

Teaching is *not* a thankless job. The kids bring you notes, drawings, and gifts on occasion and many parents express thanks for your efforts in teaching their children. In fact, there is a whole week devoted to thanking teachers-Teacher Appreciation Week in May! Now custodians, on the other hand, do not receive the thanks they deserve.

As teachers pack up for the summer months and get ready for a break, the custodians are ramping up for major summer cleaning and building projects. Teachers, and the public at large, don't realize the nearly miraculous fete of thoroughly cleaning, painting, repairing and updating

7 schools in our district in roughly 2.5 months, all the while working around summer school and summer teacher inservice activities!

I was one of those teachers who taught summer school in the morning and then worked with the custodians in the afternoons. I would paint the halls of our middle school after summer school let out and by doing so, I got to see much of the work custodians did behind the scenes.

Taking care of a school is much like taking care of a home, just on a larger scale. There is a constant battle between maintenance and finding better ways to do things. Heating and air-conditioning problems, electrical work, plumbing work, meeting room set-ups, and the relentless classroom and floor cleaning are just some of the activities custodians do all the time.

From my own experience, I saw an interesting dichotomy in the educational workplace. Either teachers and administrators treated the custodians with respect or they pretty much ignored them. From my own experience, I loved working with the custodians. I was a custodian. A new teacher to our building, who was a tad aloof and grumpy, first saw me as I was painting the hallways during the summer. When she saw me seated with a bunch of other teachers at the first faculty meeting of the new school term, she thought, "What's *he* doing here?! They let *custodians* sit in on faculty meetings?!" I had a lot of fun with that one for a long time. Still do.

Custodial work is not easy. Just try replacing your own kitchen faucet sprayer, when you have 2 inches of work space behind your sink and three inches of fingers. You get my point. After a few years of summer painting by myself or with student helpers, I convinced a fellow teacher that summer painting was not such a bad gig. It was only four or five hours a day in a mostly air-conditioned working environment. We could listen to music, drink Mountain Dew, etc. Well, he bit, and we became a painting team. The very first day he joined me, I was so excited to show him the ropes. I loaded up the rolling scaffolding cart with all the necessary materials: paint, screwdrivers, blue tape, paint-splattered radio, five-in-one tool, FPMD (Full Power Mountain Dew-all sugar, all caffeine), etc. I laid down the red rubber painting tarp in the hallway, pulled out a few brushes, filled the roller tray with fresh white paint, all the while briefing him from my vast knowledge on the basic practices of professional painting. I then proceeded to step backwards onto the roller tray and splash a gallon of white paint all over the terrazzo floor, onto my pant leg, and halfway up the adjacent lockers! Thus ended my first and last painting lesson.

No, custodial work is not easy. It's kind of like screaming at the refs during a basketball game. With our instant and super-slow-motion replays on tv, we think it's so easy and we know all the calls. Until you've officiated anything, just hold off on your criticism. Put on a whistle and try to make any kind of call on the court, live. It is quite difficult. Same with custodial work. Until you've grabbed a broom, paint brush, or screwdriver and done it yourself, hold off on your criticism of others.

Custodians work hard day after day and I think they enjoy seeing frazzled teachers buried behind mounds of paperwork at their desks after the end of the working day. It reminds them they don't have to interact with people too much on the night shift, and when the clock hits eleven, they're going home with nothing under their arms. Every job has its advantages and disadvantages.

Having spent many a summer afternoon rolling paint onto what seemed like endless hallway walls, you can imagine that the mind can drift a bit. As a matter of fact, the mind screams for activity and like a weed sprouting up from a crack in the middle of a Walmart parking lot, humor finds a way to make tiresome tasks palatable. Custodians like to have fun and ribbing each other is prerequisite for the job.

One communication technique I learned working with the full-time custodians was to assume your buddies know less about repairing a problem than you do. You could hear things like, "What on earth are you doing?! Here, let me show you how to do that!" or "Where'd you learn how to do that, in the circus?" It's fun to act like you're the expert and no one wanted to admit they didn't know how to do something like fixing drinking fountain valves or replacing ceiling tiles. This attitude brought about many moments of humor, especially when "the expert" took over and quickly proceeded to screw the job up worse than it was before. Even then, you could always blame it on the district! "Why doesn't the district ever buy top-of-the-line tools?! Always skimpin' on the budget. Damn crapperware!" Even with the joking and maybe because of the ribbing, the fountains always got fixed and the ceiling tiles were seamlessly replaced.

I experienced the lack of respect custodians may feel from time to time and I'm as altruistic as the next teacher, but even I have my limitations. Case in point . . one fine summer afternoon, whilst in the middle of painting the wood shop walls, a parent of one of our former students caught my painting companion and I in the doorway as she was showing her daughter her new locker and practicing combinations. She was surprised to see us in painting clothes and wielding brushes. The conversation went something like this:

"Hi Mr. Shurilla and Mr. Schmidt. You guys paint here during the summer?"

"Why yes, we do!"

"Well, I guess that gets you up and keeps you busy!"

"Sure does."

"Do you get paid for this?"

An awkward pause and moment of silence.

"As a matter of fact, yes. Yes we do."

"Awesome. Have a great year. Bye!"

Perhaps I am too small. Perhaps my ego wouldn't fit, even in a distorting circus mirror. Perhaps Mother Theresa's picture doesn't hang in my hallway at home, but come on here, folks. *"Do you get paid for this?!"*

"No, I don't get paid for this! Are you kidding?! Who would pay to have this done?! I don't have *anything* better to do on summer afternoons than haul around ladders and tape the bottom edges of endless hallways. I *love* rolling and brushing miles of paint. Paid for it? Well, maybe if Charles Ingalls from *Little House on the Prairie* bartered with me, I might paint in exchange for a pork butt, but money? No way! *You* love it when you get the chance to paint a room at home, don't you?! Well, how blessed am I?! I get to paint classrooms and hallways *every day!* Paid for it? Just to slap on paint?! No way, my friend. I'm better than that."

I am not better than that. Put me in a donkey suit and spray paint "Cheap O" on my side, but I actually *expect* to be paid for my efforts. Teaching *and* painting are work, people! During the school year, we would often use the phrase, "Do you get paid for that?" whenever work of a dubious nature came up, like coaching, tutoring, teaching, hauling bricks, rocketing to the moon, or being elected President of the United States, etc. You get the picture.

The sanctity of break time to a custodian is akin to a mother rabbit protecting her fuzzy newborns from a circling red-tailed hawk. Do not mess with our break! That fifteen-minute period of peace seemingly affords the only buffer between sanity and lunacy, between congeniality and hostility, and ultimately between "Okay, I'll do it" or "That's beyond my pay grade!"

One could be moving radioactive plutonium into a lead containment vessel, but if the break whistle blew, you'd drop that canister then and there, and rush to the break room for a few pretzel rods and a Diet Coke. Plutonium be damned!

The only possible way that break time could be shortened would be if you were sitting around a table in the break room, playing *Star Trek Uno*, sipping your soda, and then the boss walks in. We'd get back to work faster than cockroaches scattering when you turn on the light!

Since I'm speaking of break time, let me entertain you with a joke my dad told me many years ago when I was a kid and has been repeated *ad nauseam* in the Shurilla family ever since. It contains a punchline that works in the custodial world quite nicely and just about any other occupation. The joke goes something like this:

One day a very bad man, Mr. Walker, died and went straight to Hell (he must not have been a teacher because they didn't give him his "ignoring kids" video first). Upon entering Hades, he met The Devil who was more than happy to greet him.

"Welcome to Hell, Mr. Walker!" spewed Satan. "Ya know this place isn't as bad as people make it out to be."

"Really?" questioned our malignant sinner, suspiciously.

"Most certainly," replied Beelzebub. "As a matter of fact, we here in the Pernicious Inferno believe in free choice! You believe in free choice, don't you, Mr. Walker?"

"Why yes, yes I do!"

The Devil coughed. "Well then, let me present you with three choices. You see before you three doors. Behind each door is a Personal Hell designed with you in mind. You may choose which door of Hell to enter."

"Wait a minute here, Satan. It's no choice if I don't know what's behind the doors!"

"Right you are, my bad man, right you are. But in today's Hell, we are much more politically correct. In the old days, we'd just have you guess your door and 'Poof!' off you'd go to oblivion, but not in this day and age. I will personally open each door of Hell for you, let you take a look inside, and then you may select the door of your choosing."

"I don't know, Lucifer. This kind of has a *Twilight Zone* like feel to it."

"Well, Mr. Walker, you have *some* choice here, but you don't have *much* choice now, do you? You are in Hell after all! Would you prefer I make the choice for you?"

"Ahh, no, no, that sounds like a bad idea. Go ahead. Show me Door #1."

"As you please."

The Devil opened Door #1 to reveal a scene of fire and brimstone, with numberless bodies tied to wooden posts, burning to death, shrieking, and writhing in agony!

"Close the door! Close the door!" shouted our sinner in horror. "That was terrible!"

"So say they all," quipped Satan and eagerly added with a sinister smile, "Here's Door #2!"

Door #2 opened to a man screaming, strapped to a hospital gurney, while seven ghouls, each with a different size knife, were playfully carving his flesh without any anesthetic.

"Shut the door! Shut the door!"

"Of course. Of course. Now, are you ready for Door #3, Mr. Walker?"

"Somehow, I don't think I'll ever be ready. Go ahead, Devil. Do your stuff."

Door #3 creaked open to expose a host of poor souls standing amid a football field-sized pool of fecal matter that came right up to their chins. Only their heads showed. The Devil's minions patrolled outside the pool.

The smell was overwhelmingly vile and putrid, but there was no screaming. The Devil shut the door.

"Well," Mr. Walker began, "I definitely don't want Door #1 or Door #2. There's just too much suffering there. Door #3 is no picnic, but I guess it's the least of three evils."

"A wise choice, befitting your crimes, Mr. Walker. You may enter Door #3 and take your place alongside your fellow sinners."

Mr. Walker stepped gingerly into the putrid pool of raw sewage and stood at attention, stiff and rigid, with his chin just above the foul mess. He thought for a moment, "Ya know? This isn't *that* bad."

Just then, Satan came in grinning, looked at his watch and said, "Break's over. Back on your knees."

Imagine the good-natured ribbing you would endure if ever you were caught resting in the hallways by a couple of custodians, shouting a salvo of "Break's over. Back on your knees" imperatives your way. Ahh, what a fun-loving bunch!

Another interesting anomaly of the summer custodial work force were the high school kids who signed on as summer helpers. I dubbed them, "The Walkers." Now these Walkers have nothing to do with the previously mentioned, Mr. Walker. No sir, these "walkers" were more of TV's *The Walking Dead* kind of walkers. You know, the head twisted zombies, roaming through vacant city streets, . . . *that* kind of walker. Well, in the middle school summer work force, young walkers were aplenty.

The high school summer staff, just like any work force, exhibited all the working traits you see in adults. Some were born leaders. Some followers. Some worked their butts off and others just wanted to get work done and go swimming. I certainly didn't blame them for that, but back to the walkers.

It would begin simple enough. As the clock inched toward 1:50 p.m., the walkers would begin to appear, slowly coming out of darkened classrooms or dimly lit hallways. Their walk would be stilted and their cell phones illuminated their blank, expressionless faces. An occasional grunt, groan, or giggle could be heard as the devices pleased or angered them.

The walkers would sometimes randomly converge and bounce off each other in the hallways, like bumper cars at an amusement park, all the while their collective movement hypnotically leading them to the break room and the 2:30 p.m. sign-out sheets. Since my painting cohort and I usually painted until around 3:30 p.m., we could gauge the time of day to the minute by the first walker appearance. "There's a walker now, Paul, must be 1:50." Or perhaps we would overhear one of the custodial walkie-talkie's blast, "There's been a walker sighting in central hall; synchronize your watches accordingly."

Al McGuire, the legendary basketball coach of Marquette University and NBC Sports analyst, once spoke of the need for making "a right turn" in life. You see, McGuire lived in the suburbs of Milwaukee in a town called Brookfield. Day after day for thirteen years, McGuire would take a left turn out of his affluent subdivision and head to downtown Milwaukee to coach the Warriors. I guess many of us make a similar, monotonous day-to-day drive to work each day. We just put our brains on auto-drive and after a half hour or so we arrive. But every now and then, McGuire quipped, "we need to make a right turn." Instead of that left turn toward town and work, make a right and go somewhere you've never been before. Go out into the country and meet people. Talk to farmers sitting on their tractors in the fields. Talk to shop owners and people in the streets. McGuire said if you really want to get to know people, become a bartender or a cab driver; that's where you get a degree in life. He said, "If you really want to know what's going on at a place, get to know the custodians." In fact, when McGuire was diagnosed with leukemia, he said he went to a hospital, found a custodian, and asked, "What am I in for?"

I relate to that kind of grassroots wisdom. When I was growing up, my dad (a Marquette grad himself) was a television repairman and one day he asked if I wanted to come with him to Al McGuire's house to return his fixed TV set. You bet I did! All I remember was that Al wasn't home, but I did get to look at all the MU pictures on the wall, meet his kind wife, and get a feel that this was truly, a down to earth family.

Most teachers don't get the opportunity to work with the custodians they see everyday, busily cleaning and maintaining a safe learning environment for the kids, but I did. I guess it was like taking that right turn, getting out of my everyday grind to experience another's. My time as a custodian taught me many lessons, most notably work hard, work as a team, find a better way and have fun doing it. I guess, in a way, we were both custodians of education. And get this . . I even got paid for it!

THE ELEPHANT MAN DIARY

Most teachers have a favorite lesson or two they look forward to teaching each year. A lesson they feel totally comfortable with and one they love for its impact on kids' learning. For me, *The Elephant Man* lesson jumps to the front of the list.

I usually taught *The Elephant Man* as my first reading lesson of the school year, but if I didn't teach reading that year, I would try to work it into a special lesson somewhere in the teaching day. The story in the magazine was told in a play version, so the kids were given parts and they read it aloud. I felt at the beginning of each school term, there was a short window of time in which most of the kids were a little bit scared of the new school environment and would therefore be on their best behavior. This afforded the teaching miracle of *paying attention*. They would actually listen to the teacher more intently and try their best. I'm also a big believer in promoting a safe classroom environment in which to foster learning and that's where *The Elephant Man* lesson got us started off on the right foot.

If you're not familiar with *The Elephant Man*, let me give you a quick overview. Joseph "John" Merrick was born in England in 1862. The story is told that he was deformed at birth with massive skin tumors covering most of his body. His head was extremely large, misshapen, and he spent most of his youth being exhibited in a traveling freak show. *The Elephant Man* story is nonfiction and there are actual photographs of him in *READ Magazine*. He met a kind doctor, Dr. Frederick Treves, while in his early twenties and soon went to live in a London hospital where he received care for his condition. Merrick was a man who had been shown very little kindness in his life, was mocked, ridiculed, and taken advantage of at every turn until he met Dr. Treves.

As the story goes on, we see how different people react to this hideous creature of fate. The carnival hawker who controlled his life for so many years was a despicable fellow, abusing him physically and using him for profit. The nurse who first attended him at the hospital was aghast at his appearance and smell, but eventually grew to love him for his inner goodness and nobility. And then of course, there was dear Dr. Treves—the professional who saw a fellow human being treated cruelly and did something about it.

The reason this story was so useful to me as a teacher was that everyone, every kid, felt sorry for The Elephant Man. They felt the pain of the whippings he received from the carnival worker. They felt the shame of his own appearance when a mirror was thrust in his face. They felt the melancholy joy when Merrick, after being greeted by a famous London stage actress stated, "She was the first woman I ever met, who at our introduction, smiled at me." If they felt empathy for The Elephant Man, perhaps that would transfer into empathy for their classmates.

As we soon discussed in class, we all feel like The Elephant Man sometimes . . the one who's different, the one who doesn't quite look the same or talk the same or dress like most everyone else. It seems to be human nature to pick on the one who's different, but is that the best way to be? Can we rise above this base instinct and empathize with the outcast? Can we mature to the point where we realize we all have differences and deficiencies when compared to others and that it's all right? How many of the shooters in our schools have felt isolated and shunned by their peers? Can't we do a better job at including instead of excluding? In fact, our differences add variety and splendor to life. Most people love this quote: "The glory of creation is in its infinite diversity and the ways our differences combine to create meaning and beauty," until they find out who uttered it. I'll tell you later.

As teachers, we know that telling and discussing elicit a certain amount of learning, but *involving* students in creative ways enriches the instruction and hopefully lengthens the duration of the lessons learned. Herein lies the power of the Role Audience Format Topic (RAFT). After reading and discussing *The Elephant Man*, the students were assigned to create a journal entry from about 1890, wherein they were to choose the role of one of the characters in *The Elephant Man* story and write about one day in their lives. This was their *role*. The facts they wrote about could be true or imagined, but they had to be true to character. If you chose the carnival worker, Horace Gall, you better write in a cruel, ignorant, unfeeling fashion. If you chose to be Dr. Treves, you would present thoughts that were caring, empathetic, and protective. If you chose Nurse Somers, you would exhibit concern, nurturing, and professionalism in your journal writing.

Since this was a personal diary entry, the *audience* of their writing was any future reader of their journal or themselves, reading for reflection. The *format* was, as previously mentioned, a diary entry. The *topic* was simply, *The Elephant Man*, or perhaps more intuitively, bullying, harassment, and tolerating personal differences.

Although it was a homework assignment, most kids really got into it. Some students would burn their paper's edges and crinkle it up to simulate an aged document. Some would type, others would hand-write it out. But what the assignment did was solidify in the students' minds that teasing is not okay. It hurts. Once harsh words are said, there's no way to take them back. We all have feelings. We're all imperfect, but we all have the ability to rise above our limitations and treat others with kindness and respect. Kids this age are growing so fast and changing constantly. They need to conceptualize and think about how their words and actions affect others. By beginning the school year with *The Elephant Man* diary project, we were reminded to be kind to each other and that everyone deserves respect. In *The Elephant Man*, John Merrick utters the words, "I am not an animal! I am a man!"

Each year, I collected a few of the students' diaries and put them into a booklet that I would show each new class as examples. Sometimes the students would add pictures to their journal entries which always brought a smile to my face for I love student artwork One year, an extraordinary student made me a complete Elephant Man Diary book! She included not just one day in Merrick's life, but over a week's worth of journal entries.

I also had the students read their diary entries out loud and minimally role-play their chosen characters in front of the class. On the day we read them aloud, I told them they could add any vocal accent or dress up like they think their character would have dressed. I turned off all the lights and positioned the overhead projector (see dinosaur teacher definitions) with the light blasting them from one side creating a mysterious dark/light contrast on their faces. I told them this symbolically represented the good and evil of the characters they were portraying.

This was also a good way for all the kids to get to know each other at the beginning of the year. Since everybody *had* to read their journal entries in front of the class, it safely forced them to come out of their shells a little bit. Of course, we practiced appropriate audience behavior and all students received a thunderous applause.

John Merrick. A magnificent soul hidden inside a wretched, deformed body. Are we capable, at any age, of looking past an atypical exterior and making the effort to understand the person within? Perhaps there are hidden treasures of the heart we can all unearth with a little help from the singular example of *The Elephant Man*. Oh, I almost forgot. The author of the infinite diversity creating meaning and beauty quote? None other than . . Mr. Spock! (*Star Trek*: *Is There In Truth No Beauty?* Season 3, Episode 5)

CASTLE WOLFENSTEIN

It seems appropriate at this time to give a little Computers in Education history and share one episode from my teaching career that I'd rather forget. In college, in the early 1980s, we had a 64k Apple IIe lab with green monitors and dual 5¼-inch floppy disk drives, which I thought was pretty nifty until the first black and white Macintosh computer came out. Built-in 3.5-inch floppy drive, 128k, text that could talk . . wow! That was the top of the line tech of the day.

When I left teaching in 2016, our middle school had a networked color computer and Smartboard in every classroom, four computer labs of thirty stations each, and four mobile laptop carts. And this is already antiquated. Suffice it to say, computer technology is constantly evolving and helping our kids be more proficient, informed, and bridging gaps never before seen with our handicapped populations.

As far as technology was concerned, stepping into my middle school as a first-year teacher in 1985 was like a step backward in time, even back then! Across the hall from good old N-9 was the computer lab, wherein was housed twenty-eight or so Radio Shack TRS Model 80 computers, affectionately nicknamed "Trash 80s" by the adoring public. With its lavish 48k of RAM, dual disk drives, and black and white monitor, the Trash 80 afforded frustration at all levels of personal and school computing. But it could word process and print a copy of text with a noisy dot matrix printer.

During my first or second year at the middle school, I was given an extra assignment during my prep period to tutor a boy with Emotional Disabilities. Mark was a strong, stocky eighth grader with anger issues. To say he had a chip on his shoulder would be quite the understatement. He had a cinder block on his shoulder. He was the type of kid that spent more time with the associate principal in the main office than he did in the classroom. Profanity and sexual innuendo were his first-choice weapons, followed up, if necessary, with a second course of slapping or punching. He wanted out of school in a bad way. God bless the Emotional Disabilities teachers that tried their best to reach Mark over the years. I saw them be patient, kind, loving, instructive, and did I say patient?

I have to admit, we failed as an educational community to save this boy. As a veteran teacher, I don't have the answers on how to reach a kid like Mark. His home life was abysmal. He hung out with the wrong crowd. He *was* the wrong crowd! As teachers, we can reach many of the struggling kids and give them a redirection in life—a life with hope and purpose. But we are not everyone's miracle worker. We simply do our best, every day. It's our job. We get paid to teach and reach . . and we don't win every game.

Back in 1985, I was altruistic, inexperienced, and passionate—not the mellowed out, wise, veteran professional educator that I am today. Sometimes instinct, not experience took over. When I was working with Mark during second period every day in the IMC (Instructional Media Center), I would tutor him in math or writing or help him get caught up on his plethora of missing assignments.

Since Mark was not the most motivated of students and would rather talk about who he beat up or why he got kicked out of so-and-so's class, my task was a daily ritual of trying to keep him focused for a few minutes and at least complete some form of classwork each day. That's where the computer came in! There was an Apple II+ computer on a rolling cart in the library that I had access to each day. I would often propose to Mark that if he would complete a math assignment or finish a report in English, I would let him play a computer game of his choice for ten minutes at the end of the hour as a reward. At the time, I had never heard of *Castle Wolfenstein* and I had no idea where our floppy copy came from, but none of that mattered. If Mark asked, "Can I play *Castle Wolfenstein* if I finish page 160 in math?" I would postpone the Second Coming of Jesus. Anything to get Mark to finish a page in math!

So just what was *Castle Wolfenstein*? Today's kids would laugh at the simple 8-bit graphics and scratchy, nearly indecipherable sound bytes from the game. *Castle Wolfenstein* was a first-person shooter game, with black and white stick figure graphics. When playing, you were basically a little concentration of white lines (an English spy) chasing more white lines (Nazi guards) in a *Pac-Man* like maze shooting white dots that made scratching sounds. Sounds pretty antiquated, I know, but if it motivated Mark to get some math problems completed, it was a sip from the Fountain of Youth to a nonagenarian.

One not so illustrious day, Mark and I were seated in a small classroom in the IMC, engaged in our daily verbal skirmish over which math problems to do, and how many minutes of *Castle Wolfenstein* were on the bargaining table. I don't remember the exact discussion that took place or how many problems he completed, but near the halfway mark of the session, Mark stood up on the opposite side of the table and said something like, "I'm done with this. I'm going to the office. I feel like bothering the secretaries for a while."

That's when I got mad and said, "No you're not, Mark. I don't care if you finish any more problems, but you're not going to bother those ladies today. Not today. We're gonna give them a break."

Mark had a devilish smile on his face and I knew why. He was going to bull rush past me toward the open door and run straight to the office. Like I said before, this was thirty years ago and I was a young buck who could get worked up pretty quick at impudent kids. The only thought that kept running through my mind was, "I'm not gonna let Mark ruin another day for those secretaries. At least, not this period. I'm gonna give them the priceless gift of peace for a few more minutes!"

Sure enough, Mark bolted around the table and ran for the door, I beat him to it and simply lowered my shoulder and blocked him back. He was quite surprised at this show of force in a public school and like an angry panther, he snarled, paced back and forth along the rear wall of the room for a few minutes, gathering his will and waiting for his next opportunity to pounce at the door. He came again. I blocked him back. He paced and came again. I blocked him back. "Why are you doing this?" he asked.

"I just want to give the secretaries a break from your trash talking, Mark. That's all. Why don't you just sit down and wait for the end of the period."

He came at me once or twice more and each time I simply blocked him backward. Nothing more. He eventually calmed down and sat in his chair. When the period ended and the bell rang, I let him pass through the door and onto his next class. I don't remember much of what happened the rest of the day, but there were no more behavior altercations and Mark never went to the office . . at least, that day. I'm sure I talked to his Emotional Disabilities teacher about the incident and she would've said I should never get physical with a student. I would agree with her now, but when you're a young teacher and not used to such blatant insubordination and disregard for respect, you may sometimes act impulsively not prudently.

I actually had a pretty good relationship with Mark. There were no more door blocking hijinks for the rest of the year and Mark moved onto high school. A few years out of high school, Mark was in prison for burglary. When he was released, he met up with a few of his prison mates at a nearby cabin, they got drunk, pulled out some guns, and Mark was shot to death. Game over. Life over. Life wasted.

Teachers don't win every game. Neither do parents. Neither do police officers or social workers. We don't win every battle, but we never stop trying. For every Mark, there are many others who *do* make it, who do turn their lives around and show incredible resiliency through unbelievably horrid circumstances. I once asked Mark's ED teacher how she survived working every day with such a difficult population. She told me, "I pick my battles. I know there are situations I cannot win. So I choose to concentrate on the times I feel I can make a difference. One battle at a time."

Pick your battles. Wise advice from someone who has the hardest job I've ever seen. Blocking a Nazi guard from escaping to the next level of an 8bit computer game is nothing compared with trying to reach and teach an angry eighth grader every day within the four castle walls of a public school classroom.

Since I'm talking about violence in the classroom, where does a recently retired public middle school teacher stand on guns in the schools?

When I began teaching in 1985, there weren't many gun shootings in schools. Maybe that's why I wasn't afraid of Mark coming back to school the next day and blowing me away. "You won't be blocking me in the doorway anymore, now will you Mr. Shurilla?!" From my perspective, more guns anywhere means more killing anywhere, whether accidental or intentional. I don't want teacher's armed, but we must increase the protection of our children. We're the ones who lead by example. We teach students to work out problems civilly. We teach students not to get physical under any circumstances to solve problems, that there are better ways to resolve conflict than shooting. If I'm packing in the classroom, that's the example I'm setting for the kids—a constant reminder that lethal force is only a moment away from them at any time. Is that really a safe environment in which to learn? Who's to blame when the first angry sixth grader steals his teacher's gun and goes on a killing spree? Who's to blame when a teacher shoots his own student when his firearm accidentally discharges in the classroom? Keep guns out of individual classrooms!

Like anyone, I want our schools to be safe. I realize that *any* high school or middle school in America today has disturbed students capable of shooting sprees. I remember thinking after my first couple of years teaching, "Ya know, we keep sending these hostile, disturbed kids on to high school year after year. Most of them don't graduate and every other school district is doing the same thing. That means there is a whole cult of angry, frustrated young adults whose first outlet for their rage is the school system because we're the only ones who had to deal with them all these years!"

Most middle and high schools these days have a policeman assigned to them for illegal drug and disorderly conduct issues. I don't have a problem with having an armed policeman near the entrance of any school. We expect policemen to have guns in our society and to be prepared for anything. They have been trained in the proper use of a firearm and they are not typically in our classrooms, brandishing lethal weapons. After a time, an armed police officer near the entrance to any school and metal detectors to alert us if a weapon is trying to be snuck in, would become routine and help prevent the entry into our schools of disturbed shooters carrying weapons.

Besides an armed officer near the entrance, how about having a team of parent volunteers and retired teachers who have been trained on what to look for in school shooters greeting students each morning at the school entrances and being ever vigilant to protect their kids from a random attacker? I believe even disturbed, aggressive students, would think twice about attempting to enter a school armed, if they knew an armed officer and team of parents were waiting at the door every day. We do not need to arm this team of protectors. The deterrent would be in the single armed officer and the large number of adults, always on the lookout for a potential shooting threat.

I have been in many school lockdown drills in which I would corral my students in a corner of the classroom and read them the riot act that they could not make any noise whatsoever when the lights go off! I'd warn them if we really had an active shooter in the building that any peep or cough could expose all of us to mortal danger. Making sure we were all sequestered behind a little piece of blue tape on the floor, marking the line of sight from the doorway, I would lock the door, turn off all the lights, and take my place near the door. Standing there, holding my turned-off flashlight, I would contemplate how best to slam the door into the shooter if we were ever discovered. I remember a time when these drills were never done in school and I wonder how this impacts a child's developing psyche? You never really know what someone is thinking without asking them. I didn't ask. Just went through the motions of the drill, just like the tornado and fire drills we do every year. From my perspective, the lockdown drills didn't *seem* to bother them or me. As soon as the drill was complete, we would hop right back into the day's science lesson and carry on and that would be it. No student ever came to me saying he or she was scared, but as a class, we didn't discuss it. That's one thing that is definitely on my "do over" list.

The current generation of students has grown up with school shootings becoming commonplace and they're beginning to reach the boiling point. They want something done. The NRA seems to put the right to bear any and all arms above the right to have common sense. They seem to have a stranglehold on politicians' ability to legislate on behalf of the majority. Making mandatory background checks before the purchase of a gun and banning automatic assault weapons is common sense, which I believe, is the name of the papers Thomas Paine and Benjamin Franklin wrote so long ago. It will not tear in two the parchment of the Constitution and empower Big Brother to usurp control of our lives. It will simply better protect our children and hinder the access to deadly automatic weapons from criminals and the mentally ill. I don't believe we can eliminate all the school shootings in a country with so many weapons in so many unsupervised homes with so many troubled kids, but I know we can do better. We can minimize the carnage. We can inhibit the access to automatic weapons. We can better fund mental health institutions and school programs.

We've come a long way since *Castle Wolfenstein* first titillated the pioneers of the gamers' epoch. I don't know how much of an effect the video gaming revolution has had on the development of the American adolescent psyche, but can any reasonable person deny that first-person-shooter games have contributed in a negative way to the proliferation of gun violence in America?

America will soon decide. The blind lady of justice standing in front of the Supreme Court will soon be weighing guns on one scale and the lives of our children in the other. Will she continue to hold the sword of justice or will she replace it with the AR-15 she just picked up at a local gun show? We may have evolved past the days of preventing 8bit Nazis from entering *Castle Wolfenstein* on the Apple II computer, but can't we better keep assassins from storming our school hallways? I know we can.

LARRY SHURILLA

THE LUCKIEST MAN

In September of 2008, my twenty-fourth year of teaching, I was out cutting the grass in my backyard when I noticed that my right arm felt weak. I dismissed this feeling as a side effect of the anti-cholesterol medicine I had just begun taking, but the numbness didn't go away even after I stopped taking the medicine. A few more months went by and besides the numbness, my arm began to ache as well, so I decided to see the doctor.

In late January of another frigid Wisconsin winter, my doctor said the arm pain may be caused by a pinched nerve in my neck, so he prescribed an MRI. I drove to the testing facility, put the hospital headphones on, entered the torpedo tube of the MRI machine for immediate firing, and proceeded to have my neck scanned by the deafening clank-clank of the heavy electronic magnets. Once I was fully dosed with electromagnetism, I was honorably released from the medical service and headed home. By the time I got there—which was about a six-minute drive—there was a message blinking on my answering machine. I pushed the button and listened to my doctor's secretary saying it was urgent that I get back to his office immediately!

When I entered the doctor's office that afternoon, there was a look of dread on all the nurses and secretaries' faces. I was beginning to feel that something real bad was up. The doctor sat me in a chair and slid up close to me. He said the MRI had revealed a tumor in my neck that would require immediate surgery. He said the tumor had eaten away most of a few of the vertebrae in my neck and this was causing pressure on my spinal cord which was in turn causing the pain and numbness in my arm. My doctor also said he wanted to take me directly to the hospital, because if I fell, the fragile nature of my compromised neck would cause it to break easily and I wouldn't be able to move or breathe.

A lot of scary thoughts went through my mind after hearing that prognosis. Everyone was thinking cancer and that this tumor in my neck was just the first of many to be uncovered. I was crying a little bit, when my doctor put his hands on my shoulders and said, "We don't know if there are any more tumors, Larry, but this is not the end. You're a healthy man and there are many scenarios that are fully treatable."

I told the doc I didn't want to be driven to the hospital. I had lasted this long without breaking my neck on the icy sidewalks of Wisconsin, so a few more hours wouldn't make any difference. Besides, I needed to go home and get a few things in order, like calling school and arranging for a long-term sub and calling my part time job to let them know I wasn't sure when I'd be coming back. I also had to be the one to tell my wife the bad news.

I'll always remember waiting in my upstairs bedroom and calling downstairs for my wife to come up. When she entered the room, I told her to close the door. I never tell her to close the door. She knew there was something horrific going on that I didn't want the kids to hear. I had her sit next to me on the bed and gave her the bad news. Having just recovered from a terrible, year-long leg injury herself, the last thing I wanted to tell her was that I needed to go have surgery in the hospital and leave her alone to tend the kids and everything else for the family.

Kathy is one of the strongest people I know and the kindest. After a few tears, she went into, "We're gonna make it and let's get this done!" mode. From there, we told the kids, rushed to the hospital, and checked me in.

If there can be good news in this type of a crisis, I received it the next day. After a total body CAT scan, no other hot spots or tumors were discovered. It appeared this growth was isolated to my neck. The plan was laid to operate the next day, remove the growth, and brace the spinal cord in the neck with titanium plates and screws. This would require about eight hours and would entail entering from the back of the neck and then flipping me over and entering from the throat to complete the surgery. They would test a sample of the tumor midway through the surgery, and if it was cancerous, they would treat with drugs and radiation for a period of time and then schedule another day to flip me over and complete the neck spine reconstruction.

Ever the prankster, I realized this surgery would afford me a moment like no other in my life and I was ready for it. Taken from my favorite *Star Trek* movie of all time, *Star Trek II - The Wrath of Kahn*, I formed a plan to execute just after the surgery was complete . . and if I was still alive. I wanted to be like Captain Spock, near death in the radiation chamber of the engineering section of the Enterprise, his long-time friend, Admiral

Kirk separated from him by a glass barrier, uttering the words, "The ship? Out of danger? Do not grieve Admiral, surely the needs of the many outweigh the needs of the few."

Kathy told me how anxious she was, along with my friends and other family members were who gathered at the hospital during the surgery, and how relieved she was when a doctor friend, who was in the pathology lab the day of the surgery, told her the tumor was not cancerous. It turned out to be an aneurysmal bone cyst—a nasty little fellow to be sure, but not the dark cloud of cancer. The cyst was removed, and the metal plates, plastic vertebrae, and screws put in place. There I lay in the post-surgery recovery room, waiting to wake up from my anesthesia and to execute my cunning plan.

I recall hearing beeping noises in the recovery room like I was at the far end of a long hallway, but being too groggy to even open my eyes. I then heard a familiar voice, my wife, Kathy, saying something like, "Larry, wake up. The surgery's over. Can you hear me, Larry? Wake up."

Now was my time. With my eyes still closed, I gestured with my hand for Kathy to come close to me. As Kathy touched my shoulder and said, "Larry? Are you awake? Are you okay? How do you feel? Are you in any pain?"

I gestured again for her to come close to my lips. She did so and said, "I'm here, Larry. I'm right here."

I whispered, "The ship? Out of danger?"

I then heard that characteristic groan I've heard so many times in my life and she said loud enough for all the nurses in the room to hear, "He just quoted a line from some stupid *Star Trek* movie. He's just fine!" I felt completely successful. I had quoted my hero, Spock, in the most dire of circumstances and for one small moment in my quest to make dark moments lighter, I had achieved perfection. At least I thought so!

After about a week in the hospital, I convalesced at home for five more weeks and communicated with my subs and teacher friends at school about lessons and when I was coming back.

It's hard to describe how blessed I was during this whole ordeal. My wonderful wife and kids at home were great. I had so many friends with cards and visits. I especially loved the homemade cards sent from my students at school. They actually made a book of cards for me. Here are a few samples of their characteristic middle school wonderfulness:

"Dear Mr. Shurilla,

I hope you are running to recovery. Math is not as fun without you here. We will all miss you. The school is dead without you."

"Greetings Captain Shurilla,

We are doing well here on the Enterprise. Except the tribbels on board are getting real loud so we think there are Klingons aboard. Everyone is really missing you and there is an enemy ship coming in and only you can stop it because no one else knows math like you! We hope you are feeling well and come back soon. Captain Kirk is buried in tribbels! Boom!
P.S. Scottie's buried in tri . . hhh. Oh my gosh how many tribbels are there. I'm buried too."

"Dear Mr. Shurilla,

I hope that you feel better soon. I want to see you at school. I wonder when you will get back? How was your weekend? Mine was fun. I baby sat for a eight-week old baby. The baby was my little sister. Go Packers Rule!"

"Mr. Shurilla,

Get Healthy Soon! We have the awesome Mrs. Blank as a long-term sub, and it's pretty cool having her back. One time, when you were gone, we had this old guy as a sub. He had huge ears. I've always wondered if he had super hearing or if it was just a birth defect. All he did was drag on and on and it was extremely boring. At least we have Mrs. Blank though. I unfortunately don't look forward to math after second hour anymore because it's just not the same without you."

"Dear Mr. Shurilla,
I think about you when I am at school and at home. I pray for you. I hope to see you soon."

"Get Well Soon!
Once upon a time, there was a teacher. This teacher was one that touched people's lives. You could see his light shining so bright. The kids loved him so much and they all lived happily ever after because there was a teacher so great!"

"Mr. Shuriller,
Hope you get back soon. Okay, two muffins were in an oven and one muffin says to the other, "It's hot in here" and the other muffin says "Ah, a talking muffin!"

"Dear Mr. Shurilla,
You are my favorite teacher. Don't tell the others. You make us laugh and giggle. You actually teach us, I learn. Get Better Soon!!

I have always loved reading what kids have to say. Their language is so diverse and honest. You can see where they are developmentally and to me, that development is both academic and human. Some kids are scholarly and write with great grammatical accuracy and expound easily with a vast vocabulary. To these, writing is effortless. To others, putting the right words together is akin to moving ten-ton blocks of pyramid limestone by hand. Yet, some of the students with the greatest academic difficulties are the most empathetic and kindest people I know. Their words may be few and misspelled, but they contain the heart of giants. To read a sixth grader's words is a great joy in teaching. Well, as long as it doesn't involve correcting two classes' reports over one weekend.

To thank my many friends at work, I wrote a message and had a friend tack it up on a wall in the teachers' work room:

> After all the prayers, gifts, fasting, and personal acts of kindness offered on behalf of me and my family, I've been wanting to somehow express my sincerest thanks and share some of the thoughts that have been going through my mind at this momentous time in my life, with you, my dear friends and family.
>
> Do you know the story of the New York Yankees legendary baseball great, Lou Gehrig? His life touched me so greatly that I have taught my summer school students about him for many years. With all the bad examples floating about for children these days, I want the kids to have a true hero to look up to. Lou Gehrig played first base for the Yankees and was knick-named, "The Iron-Horse." He played in 2,130 consecutive baseball games in his 15-year career. Lou hit for a lifetime .340 batting average, had 23 grand slams, 493 homeruns and knocked in 184 RBI's in a single season. Lou was also a triple-crown winner. These are just a few of his records, but if you know baseball, it's hard to find anyone comparable. As great a ball player Lou Gehrig was, he was equally known as a wonderful human being. He treated others well. He loved his parents and his wife. You would not be reading in the national newspapers about Lou Gehrig's late-night exploits. During Lou's final season of 1939, he was having noticeable trouble in spring training. After only 8 games into the regular season, numbness had crept into his hands and no matter how hard he worked, things were still deteriorating. No one would dare take the Iron-Horse out of a game, not after 14 years of not

missing a game, but one day, in the Spring of 1939, Lou Gehrig went to the batter's circle, grabbed a bat and felt that numbness and said, "Coach, you'd better put someone else in." It wasn't long before Lou was diagnosed with a fatal degenerative muscle disease, ALS, later named after him- Lou Gehrig's disease. ALS is incurable and Lou knew he didn't have long to live. The man synonymous with strength and endurance would watch his own muscles slowly weaken, until they could no longer draw breath from this world. On July 4, 1939, the Yankees held Lou Gehrig Day at Yankee Stadium to honor their slugger, their hero, and their friend.

Yankee stadium was packed that afternoon as 62,000 fans, coaches, former players, family, and friends came to pay tribute to this wonderful human being. When Lou Gehrig took the microphone, clad for the final time in his #4 Yankee Pinstripes uniform, he uttered the immortal words, "Today, I consider myself, the luckiest man on the face of the earth. That I may have been given a bad break, but I've got an awful lot to live for." Lou also spoke of his loving parents and wife, how much they had always sacrificed for him. He spoke of great teammates, coaches, writers, and the fans that had cheered him on throughout his career. Yankee Stadium is being torn down this year, but those words still echo in the minds of many, many people and always will as does the image of this great, humble man, head bowed down, standing at the mic, surrounded by those he loved.

I have thought of Lou as I have gone through my own health crisis. I have little in the way of athletic skill or fame in common with Lou Gehrig, but I too, have grabbed that bat and felt the numbness in my hands. I have questioned whether my time was up on this earth and I have seen the faces of friends and family gather around me like a warm 4th of July to offer their total love and support, come what may.

When I was about 11 years old, Bart Starr, beloved quarterback of the Green Bay Packers, was honored during a halftime ceremony at a game at Lambeau Field. Here too, Starr, invoked the treasured words of Lou Gehrig as he said amid the Packer greats, that he too considered himself the luckiest man on the face of the earth. These words of my heroes have stayed with me for many years.

There have also been two scriptural passages that have been a great source of strength to me this past week and a half. The first is the 23rd Psalm found in the Old Testament. I lay this scripture open on my pillow as I went into my 8 hour surgery:

"The Lord is my Shepherd. I shall not want. He maketh me to lie down in green pastures. He leadeth me beside the still waters. He restoreth my soul." These words spoke peace to my soul. They're so clean and pure and beautiful. As I walk with the Lord, there could be no greater companion. With Him, wherever I may be, I truly never walk alone.

"He annointest my head with oil." The priesthood of my church came to me and blessed me by anointing my head with olive oil.

"Yea, though I walk through the valley of the shadow of death, I will fear no evil. Thy rod and thy staff they comfort me." I felt somewhat like a child again, humbled, and that the Lord would allow me to hold his finger because that's all I really needed at this time—just to let me know He was there.

"Surely goodness and mercy will follow me all the days of my life and I will dwell in the house of the Lord forever." Goodness and mercy have always followed me. I was raised by loving parents and my mother, now 88 still prays for me and sends me poetry. My 4 older brothers, my sister, and my in-laws have shown tremendous support and love throughout this dark time and have always been there for me. I have tread the streets of Tokyo, Japan for two years and shared the Savior's Gospel of Peace as a missionary. I have been blessed with two sons who have also walked the streets and towns of Taiwan and Japan and this Friday, I will be at the airport to welcome my 2nd missionary son home. My two other children are so talented and so good, I am often surprised that they are really mine! My dear wife, Kathy, who has borne such an awful burden these past few weeks, has treated me like a king. High School friends, work friends, church friends, neighborhood friends, each so personal and beloved . . I have seen their faces and felt their love and prayers so much these past few days. George Bailey has never had anything on me! If you look in my pocket, you might even find Zuzu's petals! Goodness and mercy? Yes, they have been my lifelong companions.

The other scripture that has given me strength and comfort is found in the life of the Savior in the New Testament. During this ordeal, I also told Kathy that I felt a little like Peter (that is my middle name you know) and how when the Lord was walking on the waters of the Sea of Galilee one night, he bade Peter come to Him. Peter started to come, but as doubts filled his mind and he turned away from the Savior, he began to sink. I told Kathy that come what may, I would keep a steady eye on the Savior and not look down at all the awful things that could be happening and swirling in the depths below, but keep my mind and spirit focused on the love and light of Jesus Christ—He who raised the dead and gave sight to the blind and made lame men walk—to Him would I keep my faith and not allow my eyes to wander in paths of doubt and darkness.

"The luckiest man . . " You will no longer hear these words echo through a hushed Yankee Stadium, nor will they float with smoky breath over the frozen tundra of Green Bay, but if you come to a certain corner in Menomonee Falls, Wisconsin with a little white fence and a big, old grey house, you will very likely hear a man on his knees, with a brace on his neck, pray, "Dear Heavenly Father: Today, I consider myself, the luckiest man, on the face of the earth. Please bless every one of my wonderful friends and family who have gathered around me and given so much to me and my wife and my children in this, our time of need. Please bless them that goodness and mercy will follow them all the days of their lives and may they dwell with you forever. Amen."

The day will come when my time on this earthly sojourn is complete and when that time is done, I know a loving Heavenly Father, will reach down, this time with both hands, and lift me from the tempestuous seas and cradle me home. And when your time is come, may I be privileged to count myself worthy to stand amid your loving supporters and honor the wonderful life you have lived, for the Lord has made us all, the luckiest man.

When I returned to teaching after a five-week recuperation period, I wanted to play a little joke on my kids to let them know Mr. Shurilla really was back. Since many of them had said they missed my humor . . well, this is what I came up with.

A friend of mine, who had undertaken a similar neck surgery years before, asked me if I wanted to borrow his neck brace. "Neck brace?" I questioned. I already had a hard, Aspen collar brace that I was more than happy to discard after five weeks and now had a simple foam one that had Velcro fasteners. Why would I need to borrow his brace? "Oh, this isn't any old brace," he said. "This one has Frankenstein-like bolts coming out of each side!"

"Perfect!" I thought. "Dr. Frankenstein's monster needs to pay a little visit to Room N-9!"

The day I finally returned to school had arrived and I wore my friend's neck collar with protruding metal bolts. The kids were all very kind and happy to see me, but the brace was causing eyebrows to raise. After morning announcements were complete, I went to the front of the room, sat on my trusty blue stool and retold the story of my neck tumor, surgery, recuperation, etc. Then I said that every now and then, these bolts on my neck brace needed to be tightened in order for my neck to heal straight and the time for the next tightening had arrived. I stood up, put both of my hands onto their respective bolts and began screwing them slowly, all the while shaking my head and howling with fake pain. You should've seen the faces on those kids. I felt like I was watching a test audience for the latest *Saw* film.

After a few moments of sixth grade horror, I started laughing, took the brace off, showed the kids that the bolts didn't even make it through the thick pink rubber, and proceeded to put on my regular, cream-colored foam neck collar. There was much groaning and complaining from the kids, but at that moment, they knew Mr. Shurilla was back—corny humor and all!

That health crisis ordeal was quite an episode in my life and taught me how fortunate I was to have my health, my friends, and family, but I also realized another reason I was the luckiest man: I was a teacher, and I loved my kids.

BUS RIDES

Many of us can picture an agitated school bus driver like Chris Farley in the film *Billy Madison*, head bobbing, repeatedly taking his eyes off the road, and looking up into his monstrous rearview mirror over and over again, spouting, "Sit down, you animals! If you kids don't get back in your seats and quiet down, I'll turn this dang bus around! So help me, God!"

In the *Guinness Book of World Records*, under the "Most Patient Jobs" category, you'll find School Bus Driver right behind Emotional Disabilities Teacher and Improvised Explosive Device Dismantler.

As a matter of fiction, in my recent psychotherapy session, I was asked by my psychotherapist to do some word association. He was rather surprised at this set of responses:

"Okay, Mr. Shurilla. When I say a word, please respond with the first words that come to your mind. The very first. Are we ready to begin?"

"Sure."

"Love."

"Kathy."

"Hate."

"Bus rides."

"Beauty."

"Summer Vacation."

"Evil."

"Bus Rides."

"Happiness."

"3:35 p.m."

"Anger."

"Bus Rides!"

"Misery."

"Bus Rides!!"

"Hysteria."

"Bus Rides!!!"

"Okay, Mr. Shurilla. I see we've pricked a bit of a trigger for latent hostility here. Let's try something else, shall we?"

While I was attending college, I had a summer job driving a school bus and counseling elementary age kids. During this time as a driver, I learned of the beauty of silence and that the decibels reached at a Seattle Seahawks football game were insignificant to the can of screams produced from the mouths of crazed kids traveling home in the enclosed, yellow metal cylinder called a school bus.

If one had somehow missed the joyful event of riding a school bus as a child, becoming a teacher and/or coach would provide that lost experience in abundance. In my case, classroom field trips along with track and cross country meets offered me the luxury of often being professionally escorted, school bus fashion.

Picture if you will, after teaching a full day, traveling forty minutes to an away cross country meet seated precariously close to a jet engine called "the team," then cheering your hundred plus runners on to victory, getting rained on in the crisp fall air, and then blissfully returning to school riding for another forty minutes next to the other engine, while one of your female athletes in the back seat totes a boom box on her shoulder, raucously leading the team in a chorus of "Pour Some Sugar On Me" by Def Leppard. I am not making this stuff up. To a teacher or coach, the only true enemy is noise, and our greatest reward, silence.

The advent of the cell phone did have a medicinal effect on the students. The mesmerizing, glowing box distracted them from shouting at their friends seated next to them for a moment and provided a sprinkling of peace throughout the bus for the old coaches to enjoy. God bless technology.

I never got into a bad accident on a bus (thank the Lord) but had my fair share of close calls and of course, the occasional mooning out the backseat windows at passing cars. I would always try to sit near the front of the bus, where the decibel readings were at their lowest.

Imagine being involved in this phone call just as you return to school on a bus from a cross country meet at 7:30 at night:

"Mr. Shurilla?"

"Yes?"

"This is the bus company. Apparently one of your athletes was mooning out the back window of the bus at a parent who was following you to pick her kid up."

"Okay, I think I know the kid who did it. I'll take care of it."

We already knew who the kid was because there was a buzz going around the bus immediately after we crossed the railroad tracks about so-and-so, who pulled her pants down and shined her cheeks on an unsuspecting car. The kids will often narc fast on their friends out of sheer excitement.

Then the coach (me) had to have a conversation with the accused, which went something like this:

"So, Luna. The kids said you were mooning out the back window of the bus."

"Yeah."

"So, did you do that?"

"Yeah."

"Why did you do that, Luna?"

"I don't know."

"You know, Luna, this behavior cannot be tolerated. It reflects poorly, not only on you, but on our school as well. We have to tell your parents, report this to the administration, and you'll be suspended from cross country for a while."

"Okay."

That's about how it went. I don't recall much about the girl in question. Just that it was quite surprising she'd do something like that in public and that she didn't seem overly alarmed about being caught. It's these kinds of incidents that make extracurricular jobs like coaching seem not worth it, but it's just something that has to roll like water off a coach's nylon windbreaker if you want to be around long enough to make a difference. If you're going to reach kids, no matter how well you plan, you'll experience this kind of nonsensical behavior and no matter how unpleasant or ludicrous it turns out to be, it's part of the job. That this incident happened on a school bus is just asinine icing on an already absurd cake!

Speaking of obnoxious bus idiosyncrasies, let me open the coach's disturbance door just a bit more and let you in on another annoying bus routine that made a yearly visit to our team. Now I don't think I ever offended the bus dispatchers over the years, but if I did, this would have been the perfect passive-aggressive payback. You see, the ordinary school bus was not built for comfort. No sir. It is the model of transportation efficiency. You can cram seventy-two kids into one of these babies. You don't need extravagant luxuries like seat belts to inhibit their bodies moving around at will. And they can take quite a beating and still be ready to bounce your guts around year after year. By the time kids reach middle school, this form of no-frills transportation is quite well known and any deviation from this utilitarian norm is considered an adolescent luxury of PlayStation proportions. Now that you understand the psyche of kids towards their beloved school buses, let me drive you to the punch line.

Diabolically, this particular bus affair would happen early in every cross country season, if not the very first meet. As you will soon learn, this early appearance would give the kids the entire cross country season with which to torment us. It would begin simply enough. Our cross country meets would be scheduled so closely to the end of the regular school day, that there would be an insufficient number of yellow school buses available to take us to our meets. The buses were already engaged in taking kids home. Under such extreme circumstances, the bus companies would dip into their vast fleet of mass transportation vehicles and cut loose . . . the coach buses!

Now a coach bus is no ordinary vehicle. No way, dude! This bus has carpeting, reclining seats, overhead storage racks, foot rests, mini-television screens, seat belts, and—hold onto your iPods—an onboard restroom! That's almost an invitation to moon!

When the convoy of coach buses would pull up to the front of the middle school, an audible cross country community gasp could be heard for miles. The onrush of air from the collective puff was enough to blow open the series of double-metal school doors leading out to the parking lot, allowing the team to scramble to the coach buses like a group of teenage girls rushing the stage at Shea Stadium to meet the Beatles. If you were straggling in the locker room and unfortunate enough not to be near the windows when the coach buses first appeared, the rapid word of mouth wildfire would spread to you soon enough. "There's coach buses outside! What? Are you kidding? No frickin way! Coach buses?! Are you sure?! Let's go check! Run!"

When the stampede had settled and all the cattle were seated in their reclining stalls, the coaches would take attendance, put their earplugs in, and head to the meet in *style*.

All of this sounds great, does it not? What could there possibly be wrong with having a little eccentricity to brighten up an otherwise dreary bus ride? Herein lies the dastardly twist. The coach buses would never appear again, not even to take us home from that first meet. The coach buses would drop us off and the drivers would tell us that the regular yellow buses would be back to pick us up in a couple hours. No coach buses? But why? The students' palates, now whetted with fine culinary coach bus cuisine, could never consciously go back to the big yellow bus rations. Once you've savored lobster, it's hard to go back to Mrs. Paul's fish sticks.

The students' motors, now primed with the coach bus fuel frenzy, would never stop asking about the return of the coach buses. Before the first meet was over we'd hear:

"Are coach buses coming back to pick us up?"

"No. They were only available to take us here."

"Will we get coach buses for our next meet?"

"Unlikely. They only run into trouble getting the yellow buses once in a great while."

"Will you ask for coach buses?"

"No. They're more expensive than the yellow buses. They only send them when they have to. Now go run your race!"

That was a quick example exchange with one student at one meet. You must remember that we had many away meets with over a hundred athletes on our team and each of them had inhaled the coach bus crack. Whether at practice, gathering near the gym after school, chance meetings in the hallways, or waiting for the bus to pick us up after a meet, the coach bus obsession would rear its ugly head and the coaching staff would be relentlessly badgered by their insatiable lust.

"Okay kids. As you know, our meet tonight is against Wauwatosa West at Greenfield Park. The meet should end around 5:30. Make sure you've got a ride home from school when we get back here around 6:30. Any questions?" Now that you have been enlightened into coaching hell, you know the first question we would invariably be asked.

"Coach, do we get coach buses tonight?"

"No, Jimmy. We only get coach buses once or twice a year. Any *other* questions?"

"Coach! Will we get coach buses at our *next* meet?!"

I guess after reading this chapter you can tell I wasn't the biggest fan of driving or riding school buses. They are a necessary evil in the education world, but as the Grinch would say, with all the "Noise! Noise! Noise!" I think it was time for this coach to Retire! Retire! Retire! Shame on me for thinking such thoughts, but I just had another punishment premonition. When I am dead and presented to the devil (after I make my door choice) and I'm getting ready to view my video, I'm certain he'll ask, "So Mr. Shurilla, did you enjoy your death and escort to hell? By the way, did you take a coach bus?"

SHURILLA GORILLA AWARDS

I'm not proud to admit it, but when I was in high school, I used to kid around with an old track buddy of mine, Jerry, on many a school night. We were young and naïve, but not quite the typical 1970s jocks of the day. We would create spectacular radio plays on our portable cassette tape players, write naughty novels, go egging and toilet-papering pretty girls' houses, snatch pumpkins growing in the fields, go caroling at the local mall in a bear skin cap and leotards, sing a serenade to a girlfriend at their work place, make up a fictional candidate named "Hawthorne Wingo" and run his campaign for student council, sing nursery rhymes over the morning announcements, and so on, but that's fodder for another book . . Suffice it to say, we had a great time and made fun of everything, especially ourselves.

Since Jerry was involved in band and track, I used to ask him sarcastically, "So Jerry, I like your letter jacket, but what do those three small letters on your letter mean?" Now the letters I'm referring to are "MGR" and, of course, they stood for "manager." Super jocks like Jerry and myself wouldn't be caught dead wearing "MGR" monogrammed letters on our letter sweaters and jackets and would make fun of those who did (I told you I was young and naïve). I've come a long way since those high school days, I hope! My own son was a manager of a middle school basketball team and all four of my kids excelled in band in high school. My daughter became a concert pianist and piano performance major in college. Take that Mr. Shurilla. Maybe being a manager on a sports team and playing a musical instrument in a band can be awesomely cool.

There has been a lot of discussion lately about the merits of participation ribbons, that such an award is not really an award after all and only waters down the ambition to strive for excellence, to win first place! That is the only true victory in a race, is it not? My old high school self would've scoffed at a participation ribbon. Here are my feelings on this hot topic, now.

I believe in winning. I never, personally, ran a race that I thought I couldn't win, even if the odds were heavily against me. A winning mindset is all important in competition. That being said, as a coach, I am in the business of building athletes. Wherever a particular athlete was at the beginning of a season, I wanted him or her to have improved by the end. If you were the fastest runner on our team, I wanted you to beat your best time and be the fastest runner in the region. If you couldn't run a hundred feet without stopping, that would be your first goal. Then your next goal would be to run a hundred yards, then a few minutes, then half a race, and then to complete a whole race without stopping. What would bring more joy to a person, winning a conference championship by one second or finishing your first ever cross country race without stopping? I think you get my point. Both scenarios would bring you great joy. When you do your best and see yourself improving, there is joy in the success. When you don't do your best, there will always be a bothersome feeling, tucked deeply inside that says, "What if I had given it all I had?"

I believe in awarding first, second, third, fourth place ribbons and so forth. A champion deserves a crown, but I also believe in awarding participation ribbons for finishing the race. "For all of life is like that race, with ups and downs and all. And all you have to do to win is rise each time you fall!"

I used to tell my kids who had earned a participation ribbon, but were disappointed in not winning a place ribbon, "Now take a look at that ribbon. That shows that you *finished* the race! You ran 2.1 miles and finished the race. Do you know how many kids your age you just beat? Hundreds! Think about all the kids at school that didn't even come out for cross country because they were afraid of losing. What was your time today? Was it faster than your last meet? Look how far you've come. I'm proud of what you've done. If you keep trying and giving your best effort, that place ribbon will come. Sooner or later, it will come."

As I was coaching the cross country team, besides the normal ribbons and certificates that all athletes earned, I wanted to hand out a special award each season. I wanted this award to be something that everyone would be capable of earning, yet I knew that in the end, only a portion of the team would merit them. I wanted an award for the kids with exemplary effort, attitude, and desire. I didn't care if they were the fastest or slowest kid on the team, I cared about their grit, their example, their determination to succeed. I called it the Shurilla Gorilla Award.

At the close of each cross country season, I would meet with the girl's head coach, and we would go through the entire roster and award any and all deserving individuals a Shurilla Gorilla award. Usually, about one third of the team earned the award. You could earn it one season and not the next. It was a subjective award. It depended on how coach and I felt about your effort and attitude that season. There were athletes that won three Gorillas in a row! There were athletes that never received one. I have the strongest feeling that if I had a list of all the kids who won three Gorilla awards in a row during their time on our cross country teams, that list would be nothing but leaders and achievers today. Desire, effort, and a positive attitude—when those traits are found in abundance, success will always follow.

I remember one season, visiting one of our best competitors in the hospital with our girls' coach. She had just undergone back surgery and lay in her hospital bed, slightly discouraged, but happy to see us. We brought her a small stuffed gorilla and a Shurilla Gorilla Award for that season. She immediately perked up. This young lady healed and went on to run four years on the high school cross country team. Desire. Effort. Attitude. She was truly a Shurilla Gorilla.

I was recently pumping gas at a gas station when a young, bearded man came up to me and said, "Hey Coach Shurilla! Remember me? I'm Jim Cross Country! How're ya doing?"

We exchanged some small talk and I learned he was going to school, working some part-time job, and had a girlfriend. Then, just before we parted he said, "Ya know, Coach. I still have that Gorilla Award you gave me years ago." A yellow piece of paper with an Apple II ImageWriter pixelated gorilla printed at the top, an athletes name handwritten in the center with two coaches' signatures at the bottom, and a short script that read, "_____ is hereby awarded this Shurilla Gorilla Award for outstanding desire and participation in Cross Country."

Yeah, Jim. You still got it.

By all means, give gold medals to the victors, but remember, participation leads to success.

PTC

The only other three letter combinations that come close to approaching the dread and fear poked into a teacher's heart by PTC would probably be R.I.P. or D.O.A. Yes, Parent Teacher Conferences inject toxic venom into the souls of teachers, especially more experienced teachers, because the cumulative effect of years of across-the-table-battles leaves a sinister psychological imprint on the war weary. Now what could be so intimidating about parent teacher conferences, you may ask? Are they not a time for parent and teacher to meet, get to know each other better, discuss academic and social progress, and make plans to improve the education of the child? Of course, they are. But permit me to let you in on a teacher's mindset concerning PTCs.

First of all, most conferences are scheduled after the regular teaching day. Before they've even begun, we're already tired from a day of teaching. They are usually scheduled for about a four-hour time block and during that time, one may expect to host twenty or more ten-minute conferences. Since our sixth grade house had about 125 students, that meant we would try to schedule 125 conferences with 125 sets of parents or more (some kids have two sets of parents), during three or four conference sessions. That alone is daunting when considering the herculean task of trying to coordinate that many people's schedules. Of course, ten minutes is a goal and many times it goes over. I remember the anxiety building up in me as I would look up at the clock and know there were parents waiting and pacing outside my door with a line down the hallway.

So there ya go . . we're already exhausted from working with kids all day, we've been on the phone trying to coordinate last minute changes to a totally booked conference schedule, and once they've begun, it seems like we're immediately behind schedule. Plus some parents are putting their "Do I really have to be here?" faces on.

When I first began doing parent teacher conferences, I was usually alone in my room meeting with parents. However, as the years progressed, conferences seemed to evolve into team conferences and this was fine with me. A team conference is where multiple teachers will meet with one family at a time. This provides parents with access to multiple academic disciplines at the same time without having to schedule more conferences and hunt down more rooms. The female teachers in my teams liked having me around as well, especially in case a particularly aggressive male parent was involved. I also felt more protected in team conferences, just from a legal standpoint. Plus I didn't have to do all the talking. Teacher harassment in a conference does occur, but not very often.

I never did student-led conferences. I am old school that way and usually liked to talk to the parents without their kids being around. I saw too much of parents belittling their kids in front of us to like kids being present. Of course, there were parents who liked praising their kids in front of us as well, but for me, the negative conferences outweighed the positive ones. It probably has to do with something I'll explain.

Let's get into the meat of conference fear. Let me begin by stating that ninety-eight percent of all the conferences I ever had were excellent experiences. There were so many wonderful, concerned, caring, kind, intelligent, and patient parents that I conferenced with over the years, one would wonder why I had any anxieties at all. I guess it has to do with the old saying that it takes thirty compliments to make up for one criticism. As teachers, we seem to remember the one bad apple in the PTC basket for years and years and all the great conferences in between don't seem to soften the effects of the wormy one.

Now the good conferences are kind of boring. I've learned to really like boring. I'm sure you don't want to read about the thousands of parents telling me how I made their kids' lives happier or how I transformed mediocre students into 4.0 Wall of Fame graduates. You want to hear about rotten apples, don't you? The conferences I will never forget are for all the wrong reasons.

For me, most conference nightmares are moments in time, not a nicely developed story. Perhaps, like an armadillo rolling into an impenetrable ball, my mind has blocked lengthy details of tough conferences to protect my feelings. So, permit me to share some not-so-splendid moments.

I recall early in my teaching career two conferences that left me with a bad feeling in my soul. During one of them, a particularly acrimonious father came in drunk and rambling about how we had destroyed his son. He claimed we had done little to nothing to help him improve and how he should take his son out of this blasted school, but he couldn't afford a different one. I remember rushing this conference along because I knew little of what we said would be remembered by this man and I had already gained what I needed to learn from this conference. The child's problems in school were nothing compared with his problems at home. As a teacher, I tried not to blame poor parenting for a child's academic or social difficulties at school. To me, it would be arrogant and judgmental to ascribe a child's problems to his parents, solely on a brief interaction at a conference or phone call. But in the case of a conference like the one just described, it is hard not to feel that a parent, knowingly coming to a conference after too much to drink, is in an out-of-control situation. Any child deserves better than that at home.

Another conference that I'd prefer to forget really caught me speechless. It was another early career conference and I recall sitting across from a parent of a student who was earning a D in math. I say "earning" because I tried to reinforce to parents and students alike that I don't "give" grades. I simply record what a student has earned. It would typically be very difficult to earn a D in my Special Education math classes or Regular Education math classes for that matter. I structured the grading so that if a student always did his or her homework on time, a C would be the lowest grade. I recall this student missing many assignments, which pulled down his grade to the D level. During the conference, the parent looked at me and said, "My son doesn't like you." A simple enough statement to be sure, not that hurtful really, but I was dumbfounded on how to respond. He didn't explain it any further and was just smirking and waiting for me to say something. Statements swirling around in my mind were, "Do you think I care? I'm not here to be liked. I'm here to teach your son. Your son is very lazy and he's mad at me for trying to get him to work. Why *would* he like me? I have expectations for him and he has none for himself."

After the initial wave of mental rebuttal passed, I remember responding something to the effect that it didn't matter if he liked me or not. I was a professional and would keep doing my best to help him do his best and achieve better results in math, no matter how he felt about me. I said I liked his son and saw more potential in him than he was now showing, both academically and athletically, for I also knew his son from middle school sports. The conference ended unremarkably, but it stuck. No teacher likes to be told one of their students doesn't like him. We are human beings after all. The criticisms we receive as teachers should be objectively evaluated and if we need to make a change, make it. If the jabs are unjustified, we just move on and continue to teach in a professional manner. Like Thomas Jefferson said to a grieving John Adams on the death of Abigail, "Sometimes time and silence are the only medicines."

Two more conferences are memorable and worth sharing. One year I was preparing for a conference and wondering how on earth I was going to tell a boy's parents that their son was an insatiable nosepicker! I mean, this kid dug into his nose like he found a vein of dilithium crystals (sorry, *Star Trek* references just come to me so easily!). Even peers were complaining to me and his other teachers that Peter kept picking his nose and eating the organic ore. I was witness to this abhorrent act of mucus mining and was, myself, revolted. So, as the conference drew near, I worried about how I could tastefully broach the slimy subject.

Pete was doing fairly well academically and that was how we began the nighttime conference. It's always a good idea to begin a conference with positive observations. After a few minutes of sharing academic progress and school chit-chat, I said I needed to bring up a sensitive issue.

"Well, Mr. and Mrs. Smith. Are you aware that Peter has a nose-picking problem here at school? Not only is he picking it, he's also eating the dried mucous in front of the other kids." Even as the words were leaving my mouth, I couldn't believe I was talking in a conference about a kid eating boogers! The parents were aghast and said they had no idea he was doing this. I continued, "Peter appears to be a very nice and sensitive boy, but behaviors like this really tend to ostracize him from the other kids and make building friendships just more difficult."

Oh, did I mention that Peter was also in attendance at this conference? Surprisingly, he was quite unfazed by the whole discussion. I mean, if you can eat your own boogers in front of a whole class of sixth graders, having your teacher talk about it in front of your parents might not be that big a deal. We said we would help Peter stop the habit as best we could, reminding him or cueing him to stop in class, but it really rested upon Peter's shoulders—or his nose really—to extinguish this negative social behavior.

You may be wondering how successful we were in our efforts to snuff out Peter's proboscis-picking problem? A few days after the conference, I was teaching a random math lesson and I noticed Peter near the back of the room, looking very intently, almost cross-eyed, at something sticking to his finger about one inch from his eyes. I turned back to the board for a moment and when I returned my gaze to Peter, the foreign object had disappeared and Peter had a huge grin on his face. The first battle seldom wins the war and often occurs without you even knowing it . . right under your own nose.

The last memorable conference I wish to share involves a young, beleaguered dad. This was a conference near the end of my career and was proof that no matter how long you may have taught, you've never seen or heard it all. You are always one conference away from astonishment. The dad began the conference by saying how much he appreciated all we were doing for his son and that his son really liked having us for his teachers. We responded with appreciation for his comments and that his son was a likeable young man with good ability, but for some reason, wasn't performing up to his potential and was often goofing around with his peers and missing homework assignments. The dad then brought his hands to his face and began to cry. He related the story of how on a recent night, his wife was upstairs whoring with a neighbor so she could make money to pay for her drug addiction. He called the cops to report her and when she came down from the neighbor's, he was so upset and violent that the police took *him* into custody. The boy was staying at his grandparents' house on and off, while either his mom or dad was in jail. The dad also said he had been taking prescription drugs for depression and that knocked him out sometimes, which meant he couldn't help his son with his homework and also led to his son leaving the house and getting into trouble with various neighbors at night.

I guess the point here is that everyone's got something. This dad was well groomed, wearing a jean jacket and looking like any normal thirty-year-old father, but underneath his peaceful exterior, pain and depression were lurking. Kids, of course, bring that to school with them. They may also appear like any other kid on the outside, perform well on standardized tests, be well-liked by their peers, and yet, they carry a burden inside that is almost unbearable and it's chewing them up. How am I ever going to teach math to a boy whose mom is a drug addict and whose dad is passed out on the couch at night? I've learned over the years, kids can be amazingly resilient. If they sense you love them and won't give up on them, eventually, you can reach and teach them.

It's a frustrating experience to know how much a certain kid has going against him and then try to teach a classroom full of other kids who are dealing with various issues of their own. I would sometimes look around the room and think to myself, that girl has the lowest reading score I've ever seen, that boy's dad is an alcoholic, that girl bullies everyone she can, that kid is so lonely, that kid hates his brother, etc. Then in that same room I could say, that boy's mom is the kindest woman I've ever met, that girl is the brightest math student I've had in quite some time, that kid never stops smiling or helping other kids, that kid's dad will not let him fail, etc. That is public education—the haves and the have-nots, all mixed up in the same classroom, each wanting attention, whether positive or negative, and each trying to figure out their place in school, in their family, and in the world.

In the end, I felt it my job to love them. Yes, I'm a math teacher or a science teacher, etc. I'm paid to teach curriculum, but in my heart of hearts, curriculum be damned. I wanted to give these kids a happy period at school. Their life may be a chaotic mess, but for this one hour, they'll feel love and respect and they'll know that they are somebody. Learning is one of the intrinsic joys in life. When a kid learns something new, he or she is happy. They feel accomplished. They feel pride in themselves. They feel growth. They feel hope. My job is to give them that opportunity every chance I can.

After a long night of conferences, I would often sit in my car for a few minutes and think about all those families I just had a peek into. It certainly helped me empathize with the kids and better understand what they were dealing with, which definitely made me a better teacher. And hopefully, the parents went home as well with a little better glimpse into their own child's development and the teacher who was doing his or her best to reach them.

As the clock neared the appointed hour for the end of conferences, the principal would come on the loudspeaker and say, "Thank you parents and guardians for conferencing with us this evening. Conferences will end in five minutes. If you need more time you may schedule another conference with your child's teacher for a later date. Thank you again and please drive safely." Oh boy, tell that to the three sets of parents still waiting in the hallway!

The day after conferences, we would all come trudging back to work, and look just a little bit differently at all those wonderful faces waiting for what was next. And just what *was* next? Invariably, some obnoxious teacher would pop his head in the door and say, "How'd your conferences go last night? Mine were outrageous. Hey, our next PTC is a week from tomorrow!"

Our next PTC . . .

RANGER RICK-ROLLED

Remember the number four song on Billboard's 1988 Top 100? No? It was sandwiched right between George Harrison's "Got My Mind Set

On You" and Guns N' Roses' "Sweet Child o'Mine." Hmm, still a little fuzzy, are we? Well, the opening lyrics are:

"We're no strangers to love
You know the rules and so do I
A full commitment's what I'm thinking of
You wouldn't get this from any other guy."

More clues for you. This song became an internet phenomenon. Over thirteen million Americans were duped into clicking onto phony email hyperlinks that redirected them to a YouTube video of the now infamous Rick Astley, singing his smash hit . .

"Never Gonna Give You Up"

The term associated with this prank was being, "Rickrolled!" Imagine being at a stale business conference, with your HyperStudio, I mean, PowerPoint file all uploaded and colorful. You welcome your eager audience, impatiently hanging on your every word. After showing a few monotonous slides of yearly corporate yields, you say something like, "Now here is the clincher, gentlemen and ladies. Here is the key to increasing your productivity in urban community waste management like never before. Okay, click on the link, Bill."

And then appears our hero, Rick Astley.

"Never gonna give you up, never gonna let you down.
Never gonna run around and desert you.
Never gonna make you cry, never gonna say goodbye.
Never gonna tell a lie and hurt you."

The businessman in our example might have a different opinion, but I love it! That scenario was carried out millions of times all across America. It happened to me at school, when I clicked on some link in an email and got Rickrolled. The prank became so ubiquitous in our American culture that Rick Astley actually performed "Never Gonna Give You Up" at the 2008 Macy's Day Parade, twenty years after the song came out!

At my middle school, where we like to do things old school, I initiated the devilish prank of Ranger-Ricking, Ranger Rick-Rolling, or if you prefer, being Ranger Ricked. For the concise among us, just being "Ricked" would do.

Ranger Rick Magazine is the oldest children's nature periodical published in America, dating back to 1967. Coincidently, that is just after the first season of *Star Trek*! *Ranger Ricks* always have an attention getting animal picture that fills its cover with fangs, tusks, pinchers, quills, or eyeballs that excite some, horrify others, and generally disgust the masses. Thus, it is the perfect candidate for Ranger Ricking.

It begins simple enough. Get ahold of an old, worn-out copy of a *Ranger Rick Magazine*. No, you cannot use a current *Ranger Rick* you find lying around; you have to find one of the older devils . . Tasmanian Devils, that is. You have now completed Stage One!

Once your vintage late eighties to early nineties *Ranger Rick Magazine* is selected, you will surreptitiously place the magazine into an unsuspecting teacher's classroom. Now the placement of the *Ranger Rick* is all important. It must be positioned in such a place as to avoid immediate detection. I found the *next* page in a teacher's lesson plan book to be an ideal location. Being hidden under the current day's lesson page, when the teacher turned the page, he or she would find a crazed vampire bat or agitated muskrat staring back with glowing eyes and foaming teeth. Once the initial instinctual shock passed, the teacher would then realize he or she had been successfully Ranger Rick-Rolled, and their brain would begin its algorithmic calculation as to how and when the "Rick" was placed and how they would in turn, return the magazine to the likely perpetrator—in most cases, me.

Hours of good-natured fun with clandestine marauding around the building took place as teachers poked their heads into other teacher's classrooms, hoping to find an empty room and a temporary, yet secret new home for their beloved *Ranger Ricks*. If one was really on a roll, one could access the classroom's white board and also deliver a "Today is a Free Day!" message and offer the teacher a daily double!

About a year after I retired, I received a thin package in the mail from Guelph, Canada. Now, I don't know anyone from Guelph, Canada and I did not order anything from Guelph, Canada, nor do I even know how to pronounce Guelph, Canada! Yet, the package arrived and with eyes wide and fingers eager I ripped open the envelope and found . . a vintage 1989 edition of a *Ranger Rick Magazine* featuring a screech owl snapping its jaw to scare away some pesky jays. I've been out of the classroom for a year and I'm still getting Ranger Rick-Rolled! A former teacher friend of mine and high-speed motorcycle racing champion admitted the following on Facebook after I posted an anguished request for the culprit to reveal him or herself:

"I didn't want your Ranger Rick to live out the rest of its days in my attic, and just sending it from Waukesha (WI) wouldn't have been fun, so I took it on my latest adventure to Guelph, Ontario. I'm glad it made it home safely! I couldn't let Ranger Rick quietly return to its rightful owner! It HAD to be something sort of spectacular! I've been meaning to take it with so many times when I traveled, and always forgot .. not this time though."

Well comb my mullet, put the cassette tape in, and start playing *Never Gonna Give You Up*, because I had truly, been Ranger Rick-Rolled for the ages! One regret I harbor with mixed emotions is that I was never able to plant a *Ranger Rick* in our principal's stack of in-service materials and have her stop in the middle of a presentation and pull out the picture of a wobbling wombat and say, "How did this get here?"

Here's another confession: I recently passed forward the screech owl *Ranger Rick* to the new associate principal at my old middle school. The return address included Rick Roll as the sender and the address was the Milwaukee County Zoo.

Did you know wombats are short-legged, muscular, quadrupedal marsupials that are native to Australia? I didn't think so. See, those *Ranger Ricks* are not only visually stimulating, they are educational as well!

You know, I think I'm never gonna give up, Ranger Rick-Rolling people!

ROOM N9

THE MANTIS PARABLE

Somewhere in the middle of my teaching career, I came across an eight-minute short film titled *The Mantis Parable*. I believe I was watching some Pixar animated shorts on my home computer, like *Bounding* and *For The Birds* when I came across *The Mantis Parable* and knew I wanted to share it with my kids at school.

February, when the Wisconsin winter had us by the sore throat and we were smack dab in the middle of a grey third quarter, I incorporated an activity with the kids to break up the monotony of the daily schedule. Kids can really be getting, not only on yours, but on each other's nerves at this time of the year and *The Mantis Parable* was for me, the perfect way to stop, take a break, and think about how we are treating each other.

Middle school is tough and having all those hormonally charged adolescents in the same room day after day can lead to short fuses and slick buttons that are pushed automatically. *The Mantis Parable* is unique in that it is an animated short film with no words. There is only a piano accompaniment for sound. Thus, the kids really have to pay attention, visually, in order to understand the plot of the movie and since it's short and animated, they stay with the plot pretty easily.

The Mantis Parable presents the story of a caterpillar who is captured and placed into a jar in the room of some sort of bug collector. No human being is ever shown in the movie. As the caterpillar wakes and looks around the room, he sees a framed collection of butterflies and an assortment of pictures depicting various insects stick-pinned into a collection! This frightens the caterpillar and causes him to attempt to escape his jar by climbing to the top of a twig, only to discover he can't reach the top of the uncovered jar. He repeated attempts to jump to the mouth of the glass jar, but time after time, he fails and falls to the bottom, defeated.

Resigned to his fate, the caterpillar goes about his business, munching on tender leaves when all of a sudden, a praying mantis flies through the open window into his room, lands near the caterpillar's jar, and surveys the predicament of the imprisoned caterpillar. The caterpillar motions for the mantis to fly to the top of the jar and somehow free him, but after the mantis flies to the top, he quickly returns to the ground and begins to taunt the caterpillar. With laughing motions and then drawing his hand across his throat to signify the certain impending death of the caterpillar, the mantis in his superior position of freedom, shows no empathy for the prisoner; rather, he mocks the captive caterpillar.

With the caterpillar now shaking his head in forlorn discouragement, the mantis turns to abandon him when a shadow suddenly appears over the mantis, followed by a loud thud and then darkness!

The next scene begins with the mantis waking inside the jar, now lidded, and his frantic attempts to somehow open the lid, but it's no use. He is now a lone prisoner in the jar and the caterpillar is nowhere to be found. The mantis then has a series of flashbacks in which he sees the caterpillar pleading for his help and his own cut-throat response torments him as he sees it over and over again.

The scene shifts and after a time, a glowing butterfly flies through the open window and surveys the scene of the trapped mantis. The butterfly leaves, then quickly returns with a swarm of lightning bugs, who magically unscrew the jar's lid. The butterfly then enters the jar and cradles the mantis into his arms and flies out the open window to freedom.

The end.

After watching the video, we then had my favorite part of the activity: a group discussion. Kids are so perceptive and guileless. I loved their responses to questions like, "Where did the butterfly come from? How did the caterpillar feel when the mantis laughed at him? Have you ever felt like that?" And my favorite questions of all, "Why did the butterfly help the mantis? Could you have forgiven the mantis? Do you think the mantis changed after this experience?" We then moved the discussion from insects to the students themselves. "Have you ever felt picked on? Do you remember a time when someone forgave you even though you didn't deserve it? Can bullies ever change?"

Invariably, each discussion group would give responses like:

"I remember being picked on in grade school and my best friend helped me."

"I forgive my baby brother all the time and there is no way he deserves it!"

"I don't know if bullies can ever change. They're just so mean!"

"The butterfly helped the mantis because he's kind, like me."

Following the group discussion, we had the kids complete a summary activity. On a worksheet, they were asked to describe which character they connected to and how this story relates to their lives. Most of the kids discerned that the caterpillar had metamorphosed into the butterfly and was somehow able to forgive the mantis and help him. This is not an easy thing to do, but it does show great character, the kind of character to emulate, the kind of achievable character that is the pinnacle of human morality. The kids get it and they want to become like the butterfly. In our crass, ubiquitous world of Twitter diatribes, dysfunctional cable families, and viral YouTube vulgarities, kids innately crave to be taught empathy, forgiveness, kindness, and that this is the norm for appropriate societal behavior, not the exception.

You may be thinking, "Does it really do any good to have middle school kids participate in this type of activity? Isn't this just fluff? Aren't we just wasting valuable class time when we should be enriching math or science lessons?" Here's my take on this particular curricular debate.

I believe kids should be saturated in *goodness*. They should see, hear, read, touch, and take part in goodness every day. We, the educators, should provide an environment where they want to come to school every day. How am I defining goodness? Honesty, virtue, kindness, forgiveness, patience, integrity, diligence, etc. I believe a child reared in goodness will be more likely to have strong self-esteem as an adult and have a greater capacity to learn just about anything and contribute to society at home and in the workforce. Learning is an intrinsic motivator. I used to have a poster on my bulletin board with number one on my list of rewards for studying hard:

YOU WILL LEARN!

There is no teacher alive who has not seen the look of joy that comes on a kid's face when he or she has learned something new, when the struggle of figuring something out is finally rewarded with understanding. Yes, the lightbulb will go on and a feeling of accomplishment provides the illumination. Besides the mandated math, science, social studies, and

English instructions, students need the constant influx of virtuous role models and honorable lessons in the classroom.

For those who argue these traits must be developed at home and not at school, I say this: The home is where all education begins. It is the most integral part of a child's lifelong development. School is an assistant to the education provided in the home. "Goodness training," for lack of a better term, is not mutually exclusive. It should not be done at home *or* at school. It should be done at home *and* at school. Classrooms are microcosms of the family. For a time each day, teachers are foster parents and the kids are their children. Classrooms should reflect the morals of our society and also reinforce them. We do not teach religion in the public schools, but we should teach what our Founding Fathers labeled, "public virtue." As long as the majority of our society is law-abiding and virtuous, our society will stand. If the majority is not virtuous, society will crumble. Public education has long been a foundation stone of American society, an integral thread in the fabric of our citizenship, civility, and humanity. Any way we can support public education, monetarily or with our personal time, is an investment in a stable society. Ignoring or cutting back on the needs of our public students is fools' gold. Taxes may go down a few dollars for the frugal taxpayer, but even a frugal taxpayer knows you get what you pay for.

The pendulum of education is an ongoing discussion. There seems to be two extremes in education, with rigorous curriculum at one end and social development at the other. Whenever we bury the needle at one end of this spectrum, we do the kids a disservice.

I know as teachers, we have often griped about having to teach what should have been taught at home. I know as parents we gripe, what are they teaching in that school?! Here is where we need to come together. Both teachers and parents are human; we all make mistakes, but we should always be looking for ways to better educate our children. If the pendulum has swung too far in one direction, let's pull it back together. From my experience in the middle school, at this time the pendulum has swung too far towards rigor and too far *away* from nurturing our kids. Perhaps it's cliché and an overgeneralization to say that all kids are going home and spending five or six hours every night with first person shooter games, stealing cars in *Grand Theft Auto*, and binge watching *The Walking*

Dead, but if that is beginning to sound truer than not, those formative childhood years are being wasted, or should I say *conditioned* away. Take that desensitized child, amp up the academic rigor, take out or cut back art, music, Phy. Ed., and classroom activities that promote virtue and we have the recipe for societal dysfunction.

Kids aren't watching Wally and The Beav anymore. Clark Gable's, "Frankly, my dear, I don't give a damn," wouldn't raise an eyebrow today. Let the schools help families create a climate of goodness for our children. Let them develop and implement classroom activities that promote public virtue. Let the discussion continue about where the pendulum of academic rigor/social development is currently at and let us work together to love and educate our children in the era of the greatest information and learning tools in history. Like one of my students stated in her *Mantis Parable* summary:

"My favorite part was when the caterpillar waves hi to the mantis. This compares to me because I like to have a perky spirit so I say hi to people I don't know. I think the caterpillar is like me because he is looking for opportunities."

Let all of us in the world of education look for opportunities to not only say "Hi kids, let's get going on multiplying decimals!" but also "Good Morning, Sally, you look kind of down today. Is something going on? How can I help?"

You never can tell what those caterpillars are going to turn into.

STANDARDIZED TESTING

When I was a kid, we used to take the Iowa Test of Basic Skills standardized tests. We'd get the thick paper booklets and for about one week of school, scratch our heads, look at the clock, fill in the bubbles with our No. 2 pencils (they better be No. 2s young man!), look at the clock again, and pray for recess. As I became a teacher and sat on the other side of the testing process, my attitude changed. I didn't pray for recess anymore; I prayed for the good Lord to take me home . . my Eternal Home!

You may be thinking, "Is not administering a test, 'a gift from God' for a teacher? Put your legs up on the desk, Mr. S., lean back in your chair, and get ready for a nap. The kids are actually occupied for a few minutes. Take it while you can, boy! *This* is your Christmas bonus!"

Of course, there is an appealing quality to standardized testing in not having to prepare regular lessons during those periods, but get ready for education's version of the bait-and-switch. Without getting into the merits or disparagements of the *concept* of Standardized Testing, let me share how *administering* the last testing session of my career transpired and may have been a prelude to my personal teacher's hell video.

Having morphed from handing out boxes of alphabetized testing booklets early in my career to handing out numbered laptops from rolling carts near the end, one would think through advancing technology, that this process had been simplified. One would think.

My final standardized testing sessions began as usual. We held a meeting of proctors a few days before the testing was to begin and got a peek at the testing matrix of rooms, teachers, labs, carts, times, and guidance counselor availability for TAS (Testing Anxiety Syndrome). Okay, I made up the last one, but *I* could've used it! Having studied the Rosetta Stone for decades and using my portable scanning electron microscope, I was able to decipher with some difficulty when and where I was supposed to pick up the laptop carts for my testing sessions. But knowing the plan and executing it were two different beasties.

We had already undergone an in-service on what the new computerized tests would look like and how navigating a track pad or mouse might prove problematic to some of the kids, but we were reassured not to worry. These kids nowadays are so computer savvy, they'll have no problems! Because we were still in somewhat of a transition from booklets to computers, testing stations had to be assigned. With over 1,000 students in the building, we had to stagger the use of computer labs and laptop carts to enable all the kids to have access when needed. Sounds simple enough. Just assign the computer labs and mobile carts to various classes and voila, technology wins! No more cumbersome boxes of testing booklets. No more months of waiting to get results. Wait, it still takes months to get results because they have to wait for loads of data from all over the country to standardize the results. Okay, but still, no more forest scalping booklets or No. 2 pencils to deal with!

Being the kind, easy-going, and selfless teacher I am, I offered to take the oldest devices for my testing sessions. Well, maybe I didn't volunteer for the crappiest laptops, but the powers that be knew I wouldn't complain much so I got the booby prize of obsolete electronics. I didn't care about the ease or dependability of a built-in computer lab. I didn't squabble over the latest Chromebooks with their longer battery life (future readers will certainly scoff at all these options). No, I *chose* the oldest laptop carts with thirty total laptop computers in varying degrees of obsolescence. Besides my basic altruistic nature, in this matter, I guess I was just kind of dumb.

Since I was sharing these carts with another grade and a different testing period, I would have to personally pick up the carts from another room on the other side of the building and hope the laptops had been charged again after the preceding testing sessions. Since I was teaching right up to the point of testing, I would have to leave my room unsupervised while I strolled on down to the other class on the other side of the building and picked up the rolling tank-like carts and bulldozed my way back through the busy hallways to my class, hoping no one had been strangled while I was gone.

Once the carts had been sequestered and delivered, I now stood in front of my classroom, ready to begin disseminating the aged laptops. I already began to feel the pressure of falling behind. I knew the computer labs were humming along, logged in and undoubtedly taking their first tests. The classes with Chromebooks were already frantically clicking their computerized answer bubbles and here was I, still handing out twenty pound laptops to twenty-eight impatient sixth graders.

Oh, I forgot to mention, just as I finished handing them out, a couple kids raised their hands and said, "Uhh, Mr. Shurilla, the battery bar on my laptop says three percent."

The kids were slowly powering up their computers, and I mean *slowly*. It took a few minutes just for the computer to power up, then it took the kids a few more minutes to find the hidden testing icon on the computer desktops, then it took a few more minutes to log in using the special new passwords created for each student. My worst fears soon came to fruition. It became apparent that not just a few of these computers were recently used and that dang Energizer Bunny was nowhere to be found. They were ready to power off randomly like popcorn popping throughout the classroom. My brow's furrowed wrinkles were getting deeper by the minute.

It was then I made my first impassioned plea to the IT Department. Some may think IT stand for Information Technology. No, my wise friend, IT does not. IT stands for Ignoring Technology. The IT Department was not answering my emails. They were already swamped with other teachers' issues throughout the building. I began to panic. I emailed the front office secretaries (they get everything done anyway!) with an IT S.O.S. and they said they'd get ahold of them and send someone down to my room ASAP. I love the secretaries!

By now, some kids were finally into their tests. Some were still waiting for the laptops to finish the booting process. Some sat stupefied, staring at a black screen. Others were depressed at not being able to speed ahead of their peers, and still others were beginning to sense the incomprehensible joy that they just might get out of testing today! Not so, my young intellectuals, not so. The nation's best team of testing professionals was now assembling in my room and they were prepared to dash any hope of testing postponement.

Let me offer some defense of the IT Department . . just a little. They had included with the rolling carts a few power strips in case laptops needed to be plugged into a wall socket in an emergency. Sounds legit. If they run out of power, just plug the babies in, right? All I had to do was make sure the failing laptops were near enough the two outlets in the classroom for power strip hookup and away we go! The only problem is that the power strip cords were about two feet long and after the laptops had their plug-in power cables connected, we had to move the heavy science tables closer to the wall in order to have the power cords reach. Now that's just fine and dandy for the two or four laptops that took up all the space of the power-strips, but with about fifteen laptops on the blink and the rest moments away from shutting down, picture the scene:

Some kids blissfully testing. Some kids near the wall, gloating at all the electricity flowing through their plugged-in laptops. Some kids, hands waving, watching their screens dim, and losing data faster than they could eat a fried Twinkie. And there in the corner, humming, while hugging his knees and rocking in the fetal position was good old Mr. Shurilla, waiting for the IT Search and Rescue team to arrive.

And arrive they did! Like starving wolves on the scent of a gored goat, from all corners of the building, kids from technology spoiled teachers were sent bringing a laptop here, a Chromebook there. The IT team brought backpacks stuffed with the usual electronic emergency equipment: power strips, battery packs, pocket protectors, PEDs, Hostess Sno balls, straight-jackets, Captain America fidget spinners, cyanide pills, etc. I think the IT Department has its own "Broken Arrow" alert.

Kids were actually finishing their tests in the class next door, while some of mine were just beginning to log in. Meanwhile, I was still rocking and drooling in my corner, quietly waiting for the Allstate Mayhem commercial guy to show up. Come to think of it, that one IT guy looked a lot like him ..

"This too shall pass," an old friend used to say, and like a cat coughing up a furball, this testing period did as well. Although half my class had to be retested on another day, we all came out of the testing triage relatively unscathed. Well, except for the fact that this was day one of testing and I drew the lucky straw for the old laptop carts again on day two! You know, sometimes a thick booklet with a No. 2 pencil and scratch paper can be a very comforting thing.

THE TWELVE DAYS OF MIDDLE SCHOOL CHRISTMAS

I'm not sure how it began, but a number of years ago, two of my male teacher friends and I began a tradition at our middle school of singing the "Twelve Days of Christmas" over the school's public address system on the last day of school before Christmas Break-excuse me, Holiday Break! (I almost forgot to be politically correct!) Maybe the song should be retitled, "The 12 Days of Holiday Break?!" Nope. Just doesn't sound right.

Now don't you dare picture the three of us singing the traditional Christmas carol with partridges, pear trees and women dancing. No, this was a production only male teachers could produce. Little planning, no costumes, first time is go time, and the voices were more talk-singing than anything resembling crooning. Also, the three of us did not sing alone. We enlisted an all-male staff singing review to gather in our school's main office and hand off the microphone to the next "Day of Christmas" in sequential singing syncopation. One musical instrument was present—jingle bells. And one or two of the "singers" could actually carry a tune, with the help of a middle school backpack.

The piece de resistance of the performance was the text of the song. Each year, The Big Three would sit together a few periods before the end of school and brainstorm another brilliant compilation of that school year's most notable administrative directives, in-service flops, and latest educational buzzwords from the gurus of the profession. The result was an entertaining lyrical lip-dance that even Weird Al Yankovic would be proud of!

I'm guessing we did this for about five or six years in a row before I retired, and after I left "the boys" did do one more command performance. But like all the greatest boy bands in show business history—NSYNC, The Backstreet Boys, Menudo, Bell Biv DeVoe, One Direction—the time came for us to dissolve and fade into the memories of our not-so-adoring fan base.

The only real hiccup during our performing period was the year we got a little too political. After some hefty insurance and salary cuts by our governor at the time, the mood of the teaching body was a bit, shall we say, dampened? Since the song was sung over the school's public address system, anyone loitering in the hallways could hear it . . which meant straggling students, visiting parents, etc., were listening to our song as well as the teachers and staff. Now, I don't recall exactly what was sung in reference to our governor, but surely it was not purely complimentary. One of The Big Three (not me) was called into the principal's office and the principal did make her concerns known. She also shared her confidence that politics would not enter the "Twelve Days" again, if we ever wanted to sing it in the future.

Okay, music fans, put on your Beats, plug in your earbuds, gather around the Victrola and get the "Twelve Days of Christmas" boppin' in your head. Here is one musical artifact of the great Middle School Teacher Boy Band.

THE TWELVE DAYS OF MIDDLE SCHOOL CHRISTMAS

On the first day of Christmas my true love gave to me . . .
    Doug Buehl's Taxonomy.
On the second day of Christmas my true love gave to me . . .
    Two MCAP Data Points.
On the third day of Christmas my true love gave to me . . .
    Three Diazepam Medical Training Sessions.
On the fourth day of Christmas my true love gave to meb . . .
    Four Vet's Day Community Videos.
On the fifth day of Christmas my true love gave to meb . . .
    Five House Meeting Minutes!
On the sixth day of Christmas my true love gave to me . . .
    Six Amazing Race Scavenger Hunts.
On the seventh day of Christmas my true love gave to me . . .
    Seven Google Drive Presentations
On the eighth day of Christmas my true love gave to me . . .
    Eight Aimsweb Training Sessions
On the ninth day of Christmas my true love gave to me . . .
    Nine Admin Visitations
On the tenth day of Christmas my true love gave to me . . .
    Ten Portfolio Conferences
On the eleventh day of Christmas my true love gave to me . . .
    Eleven Penetrating Math Probes
On the twelfth day of Christmas my true love gave to me . . .
    Twelve Magazine-Fundraiser-Dude Pep Rallies

While the specificity of this teaching content relates fully to my middle school, I think you can catch the tune of this melodious musical malfeasance. Merry Holiday Break to all, and to all a good night!

SHOP TALK

God bless the shop teachers. They offer a much-needed course to those boys and girls who like to work with their hands-the builders, the fixers, the creators, the designers and engineers, the craftsmen and women. To an outsider, a middle school shop class may appear to be some sort of loosely organized chaos, but an experienced shop teacher knows his work force well and he or she is able to bring order to that chaos and a finished product to an original plan.

Upon first glance, the middle school shop class may be likened to a Little Shop of Horrors. I don't mean the dangers presented by the bare bladed power saws or whirring drill presses. No, the most dangerous machines in the shop are the biological ones—the ones with acne and without deodorant. I'm talking about the ones looking to pair with their impressionistic and foolish friends in the, hands down, most dangerous environment in the school. How a shop teacher controls this group of kids is a miracle to behold and, once again, I was put in the passenger seat of the pace car.

Many years ago, at our middle school, a program titled "Integration" was initiated. The Integration Period was when a Regular Education teacher would assist another teacher in a "special" class—a wood or metal shop class, world language, art, music, phys ed or any other non-academic class (those teachers love it when they're called a non-academic class!). The regular teacher would show up day after day and plan, discipline, and help teach the special classes' curriculum. It was thought this sort of interdisciplinary mixing of teachers would bring about a more diversified approach to the standard curriculum. It was also a way to make the schedule work. I'll leave it at that. For most teachers, regular and special, the Integration Period was not the most anticipated period of the day, but we made it work and had some excellent lessons along the way.

As fortune would have it, years ago I was assigned to integrate into the wood shop class. Mr. J., the teacher of the class, was a kind, old war horse of the *The Right Stuff* era who was nearing retirement. The brightest gem of wisdom I learned from this shop teacher was how to end a class, and I'll get to that in a moment.

The shop's floor was grey painted concrete with white cinderblock walls (yes, in case you're wondering, I did paint those walls as well!). In the very center of the shop was a beautiful sprinkling fountain. Well, maybe not quite a majestic fountain, more like a circular terrazzo trough with 360-degree sprayers located in the center, misfiring whenever your foot stepped onto the black rubber activating ring. Surrounding the shop along the walls were work spaces adorned with a cornucopia of tools—wood burning pens, scroll saws, hand drills, sanders, files, hand saws, all ready to be pointed, shaken, and stabbed at any unsuspecting or suspecting student nearest the clumsy adolescent wielder. Throw in a giant planer machine, drill presses, circular saws, and electric disk sanders and you have all the ingredients for the greatest assault on hearing that man has yet devised. Walking into the shop just after the "Get to work!" command has been uttered is like a bouncer leaping into the sky near a giant onstage woofer at the opening power chord of a Metallica concert or like when your neighbor's leaf blower is perfectly pointed six inches from your face. I think you get it . . man, it's loud in the shop!

The period usually begins with the whole class meeting together to get last minute directions, answer any pertinent questions, and lay out the work plan for the period. With the "Allright! Get to work!" imperative still fresh in their minds, students disassemble and head to their respective work areas to let the war on hearing begin. Now that we've walked into the shop with machines motoring, sanders sanding, saws cutting, wood pens burning, hammers pounding, another kid squirting hand sanitizer in all directions, eight kids surrounding Mr. J.'s desk with unfinished projects and questions in hand, the time really seems to fly! Soon the clean-up bell goes unheard amid all the clattering clamor and the clock ticks toward the period's merciful end. As Mr. J. happens to look up from the student siege at his desk, he notices the near fatal time on the clock. His greasy forehead explodes in sweat and his body begins to convulse as he opens his mouth and utters a *Braveheart* freedom cry, "SHUT'ER DOWN!"

Even during this cacophony of commotion, the students are laser-tuned to Mr. J.'s vocal frequency. They raise their fuzzy brows like koalas smelling eucalyptus leaves and lethargically begin to move their equipment to the designated locations. One by one, red buttons are pushed and the symphony of shop sounds, instrument by instrument, machine by machine, begin to lose their tremolo. Students somehow manage to wash their hands in the malfunctioning fountain, gather their belongings and scramble out the door, two minutes after the passing bell has rung.

Silence. Blessed silence. At least for about the minute thirty seconds it takes for the next class to begin sauntering in.

And there you have it. Shut'er down. When the situation is in utter disarray, when all semblance of order has been lost, when the fecal matter has finally flung into the oscillating blower, "Shut'er down" restores the balance of nature. It calms the storm. It stills the teaching tempest and ultimately, it silences the integration period for one more day. Ahh, I recall the days when I no longer had integration and I'd be walking in the halls near the end of a period and above the groaning and droning of the shop machines and classroom chaos, I'd hear the distinctive charge of "SHUT'ER DOWN!" cascading down the hallways and somehow, I knew all was well in the world. Another classroom battle was won and Mr. J was bringing his troops home after another successful shop class campaign.

Nowadays, whenever life's situations seem to be getting out of hand, I remember the words of wisdom uttered by my shop teaching friend and I use them. I may only think them, but I use them. They comfort me in times of calamity. As I close this chapter, and ultimately my teaching memoirs, the resonant rant of Mr. J. rings true once more. Time to SHUT'ER DOWN!

ONE LAST LOOK

About a year before my retirement, David Letterman ended his long run from television's *The Late Show with David Letterman*. Having begun watching Letterman when I was going to college in the early eighties, we had shared many laughs over the years and of course, grew old together. As he neared the last episode of his TV career, I loved watching all his favorite guests appear before that final goodbye. Entertainers and actors, musicians and comedians, each night brought another favorite. George Clooney, Bill Murray, Julia Roberts, Ray Romano, Eddie Vedder, to name a few, but my favorite had to be Tom Waits. When Tom appeared during that final week of shows, he said he had written a song for David. As he strapped on his acoustic guitar, standing alongside his bassist and accordion player, he quipped in his gravelly voice, "This one's for you, Dave." Here are some of the lyrics to Tom Waits' song, "One Last Look."

Let's watch the sun come up in another town.
Try our luck a little further down.
Leave the cards on the table.
Leave the bread on the plate.
Put your hand on the gearshift.
Put your foot off the brake.

And take one last look
At the place that you are leaving.
Take one last look
Oh take one last look
At the place that you are leaving.
Take one last look.

Never being one to pass on the opportunity to schmaltz it up a bit, I planned on using this song when I retired the following year. As the time drew near for my last faculty meeting, I enlisted—as I had a number of times before—a few of my colleagues to form a makeshift theatrical band. The song suggested a western theme to me, so clad in cowboy hats, bandanas, a lizard on a rock and a fake campfire, three other teachers and I performed "One Last Look" for my faculty. At the conclusion of the song I played a video titled "One Last Look" which I had filmed as I walked around my empty classroom.

I began the video by opening the door to Room N-9, my home for so many years, and then proceeded to stop and glance at the walls as I

Dear Mr. Shurilla,

                I was really nervous coming into middle school. I soon later did not feel nervous anymore and that was because of you. You're my favorite teacher of all time and you always will be. You helped me become a better person and I learned a lot throughout your class. You made learning fun! I wanted to come to school because I always looked forward to your class! I hope you understand that you impacted so many kids lives. Especially mine. You were one of those teachers that everyone deserved to have, and I am so lucky to have been able to be one of your last students. I still remember the day we had a farewell party for you and that I cried really hard. You then did the thing that E.T. does to the little boy in the movie where you said, "I'll always be right there" and then touched my heart. I don't think I will ever forget that moment. It meant a lot to me. So in conclusion, I just want to say thank you. Thank you for being an amazing teacher and overall person. Most importantly, thank you for making me a better person Mr. Shurilla. I miss you deeply. Remember to always long live and prosper.

    Sincerely,
    ~~████████~~
    7th grader at Templeton Middle School
        (your favorite student ☺)

        (5/1/17)

walked around the room for one last look. So many memories are recorded on those walls—my son Keaton's kindergarten writing of a Martin Luther King quote, my authentic *Star Trek III* movie poster, student made classroom rules' poster, my brass Abraham Lincoln Memorial desk statue, school daily bell schedule, math facts' chart, my disorganized desk, etc. If you're a teacher, you know how many stories are locked inside of those mementos we have in our classrooms. I also recorded the kids saying the Pledge of Allegiance one last time and the kids asking me in unison, "Mr. Shurilla, what are you going to do after you retire?"

I responded by saying, "An old friend once said, 'There are limitless possibilities.'" The passing bell then actually rang while I was recording and I gave final, unrehearsed directions as the kids noisily headed to lunch . . a fitting end to that scene, I must say. A classroom of excited kids' talking and the bustling about of twenty-eight high energy sixth graders. If you listen closely, you'll hear one student guess correctly as to who that friend was who said, "There are limitless possibilities."

The student said to his neighbor, "I'll bet it was Spock!" Right you are my sixth grade friend, right you are.

I had one more trick up my sleeve and my friends had one more for me. At the retirement party, held at a local restaurant near the end of school, we gathered for snacks and a goodbye video that my teacher friends put together for me. In their video, our principal played me with a grey wig and slow motion raced our district superintendent to the *Chariots of Fire* theme! As "I" trip over a hurdle and fall, the camera spins and suddenly I am transformed into a walk-around-the-school-halls dream sequence dancing to Elton John's "I'm Still Standing."

The video doesn't stop there! All the number one songs from 1985 to 2016 were parodied by many staff members as I was reliving the last thirty-one years in this dream sequence of the video. I end my jaunt around the school and the music video montage amid confetti tossing and "Goodbye Mr. Shurilla" signs, by entering our old gymnasium as a bunch of eighth graders are clapping, cheering, and chanting, "Shurilla! Shurilla!"

The video was sure a hit and whenever I think back and remember fellow teachers lip synching songs like "SexyBack" by Justin Timberlake or "Addicted To Love" by Robert Palmer, I shake my head, chuckle, and realize middle school teachers are truly insane.

Remember, I am the King of the Overdone and I'll ride the circus pony until it's dead. After watching this tribute video at the restaurant, I thought about my final goodbye to teaching. How to end this great thirty-one-year run? How about a song? I grabbed the mike in the restaurant, and much to my wife and family's chagrin, I thanked all who came and helped make the video and then I sang. I told those present they would probably never hear this song sung again live in their lifetimes. It's just not the kind of song you hear performed live, and yet, it fit my feelings exactly.

I sang Randy Newman's, "I Will Go Sailing No More" from the animated feature film, *Toy Story*. I thought of changing the word "sailing" to "teaching," but then again, I thought the message was clear enough.

Out among the stars I sail, way beyond the moon.
In my silver ship I sail, a dream that ended too soon.
Now I know exactly who I am and what I'm here for
And I will go sailing no more.
All the things I thought I'd be, all the brave things I've done
Vanish like a snowflake with the rising of the sun.
Never more to sail my ship, where no man has gone before
And I will go sailing no more.
But no, it can't be true, I could fly if I wanted to
Like a bird in the sky, if I believe I can fly, why I'd fly.
Clearly, I will go sailing, no more.

It won't be long now before I have to watch my personal hell video! I hope all those kids I was too busy to give my time to, will forgive me. That was never my intent. Wish me luck! I hope it's not too long, though.

I guess it's time to get my coat and gym bag, turn the lights off, and lock the door to Room N-9 one last time. They say when one door closes another one opens. I hear the faint whisperings of new challenges and opportunities that lie ahead and yet, I know there will never, ever, be another Room N-9. My Room N-9. That was my class. Those were my kids. And like the end of another school year, I guess it really is time to move on-for all of us.

It's time to say goodbye to the custodians sweeping the floors and wave at the basketball coaches beginning practice in the gym. Walk past the darkened office with the copy machine glowing in the corner and notice a frazzled teacher making copies for the next day. Exit the building and make the short drive home. Wait, not drive home, like time . . fly.

In the future, if I'm in a casual conversation at a dinner party or chance meeting with someone in the community and I'm asked to surmise a long teaching career, the most concise and truest answer I could ever give would be, "I loved the kids."

EPILOGUE

During the first Teacher Appreciation Week that I missed due to my retirement, a kind teacher back at my building asked her class if anyone felt like writing me, their former teacher, a thank you note and that she would deliver them to me. One day in May, I discovered a thick manila envelope addressed to me from my former middle school. Upon opening the mysterious package, I was surprised to find a bunch of letters from my former students, thanking me for being their teacher and recounting some of the crazy things . . I mean challenging, inspiring, and thought-provoking lessons, we had experienced together. One letter in particular brought such joy to my teaching soul, that I thought it would be the most appropriate ending to the memoirs of my teaching career.

As teachers, we all have those special students that drive our educational passion. Whenever my teacher friends were having a tough time with terribly difficult students, I would remind them of the golden ones—the ones who come to school to learn, who are also imbedded in their classes. They are the ones who are kind, compassionate, eager to learn, and willing to help you or their peers at any time or place. These are the students that help us make it through the hard days. Their energy, their sincerity, their thirst for knowledge fuels our motivation to teach everyone to the best of our abilities. After a draining class, when you look into *their* eyes, you get recharged and gain inertia to carry on with the renewed hope that you can and do make a difference.

One day, a month or two into my final year of teaching, just after the classroom had emptied and I was looking down at my desk trying to catch my breath, I noticed a pair of eyes staring at me over my pile of books. A little girl was standing there with a note in her outstretched hand, waiting for me to grab it. It was one of the sweetest notes I have ever received. The letter read in part, "Thanks for everything so far! And now I really believe that I could be a scientist just like the Wright Brothers! I want to change the world one step at a time!" It was this same young lady, finishing up her seventh grade year who wrote me another "keeper" note. Most likely, my last. The kind of letter that makes everything in this demanding, humorous, frustrating, enriching, challenging, monotonous, spectacular, pressurized job called teaching, rewarding and meaningful. Teaching is hell and heaven, the best and worst of times. It's funny though, the more you look back, the more you only see heaven, the faces of all those kids who made it so worthwhile.

You can make a difference.

www.ingramcontent.com/pod-product-compliance
Lightning Source LLC
Chambersburg PA
CBHW020205090426
42734CB00008B/943